Museum Masterpieces:
The Metropolitan Museum of Art
Parts I & II

Richard Brettell, Ph.D.

PUBLISHED BY:

THE TEACHING COMPANY
4151 Lafayette Center Drive, Suite 100
Chantilly, Virginia 20151-1232
1-800-TEACH-12
Fax—703-378-3819
www.teach12.com

Richard Brettell, Ph.D.

Margaret McDermott Distinguished Professor of Art and Aesthetics
The University of Texas at Dallas

Professor Richard Brettell is the Margaret McDermott Distinguished Professor of Art and Aesthetics at The University of Texas at Dallas. He received his B.A., M.A., and Ph.D. from Yale University. Prior to joining The University of Texas at Dallas, Professor Brettell taught at Northwestern University, the University of Chicago, Yale University, and Harvard University.

Professor Brettell's museum career began in 1980 with his appointment as Searle Curator of European Painting at the Art Institute of Chicago, where he oversaw the renovation and reinstallation of the European Painting and Sculpture Galleries in the Allerton Building. Since then, Professor Brettell has been the McDermott Director of the Dallas Museum of Art and has advised and consulted for museums such as the Dixon Gallery and Gardens in Memphis, Tennessee; the Portland Museum of Art; and the Amon Carter Museum in Fort Worth, Texas. Professor Brettell presently serves as the American coordinator of the French Regional and American Museum Exchange (FRAME), a coalition designed to promote the exchange of art and information between regional museums in France and the United States.

Professor Brettell's museum exhibition work ranges from intimate explorations of individual artists to broader surveys of particular periods and movements in art history. His exhibitions include *Monet in Normandy* (for the de Young Museum in San Francisco); *Gauguin and Impressionism* (for the Ordrupgaard in Copenhagen); *The Golden Age of Naples: Art and Civilization under the Bourbons* (for the Art Institute of Chicago); and *The Impressionist in the City: Pissarro's Series* (for the Dallas Museum of Art). He has given scholarly lectures at numerous museums, including The Metropolitan Museum of Art, the Musée d'Orsay, the Singapore Art Museum, and the National Gallery of Art. He is also the author of more than 25 books, including *19th and 20th Century European Drawings in the Robert Lehman Collection* and *Impression: Painting Quickly in France, 1860–1890*.

Table of Contents
Museum Masterpieces:
The Metropolitan Museum of Art

Table of Contents

Museum Masterpieces:
The Metropolitan Museum of Art

Museum Masterpieces:
The Metropolitan Museum of Art

Scope:

There is no city in America—and indeed, few cities in the world—with as many distinguished art museums as New York City. Yet of all these great museums, The Metropolitan Museum of Art is the most wide-ranging and ambitious. Visitors from all over the world flock to the museum to experience its collections, unparalleled in their global and millennial scope. Since its founding in 1870, The Metropolitan Museum of Art has evolved into an influential cultural institution and a central destination for both tourists and scholars.

But how does one approach the vastness of The Metropolitan Museum of Art without becoming overwhelmed? How does one enjoy the depth of its collections while continuously appreciating the thematic connections between galleries and individual works of art? To wander blindly through the halls of The Metropolitan Museum of Art is to risk missing out on a wealth of information and history. This course offers a way both to understand The Metropolitan Museum of Art and to make sense of the wide range of works, artists, styles, and cultures that populate its various departments. Twenty-four lectures explore each of the museum's departments in depth, selecting key works of art based on their historical importance, their unique position within their respective collections, and their connections to the museum's other departments (and, in some cases, to works in other museums).

The course begins with a brief overview of The Metropolitan Museum of Art's history, from a dream in the minds of Americans eager to create a national institution of art in the United States to the iconic and ever-growing museum of the 21st century. After laying the groundwork for the course, the lectures dive into the museum's individual departments and chart a roughly linear course that takes us from the influential civilizations of Greece, Rome, and Egypt through the burgeoning art movements that proliferated throughout Europe to the disparate art styles of 20th-century artists. The early lectures illustrate how the museum's vast collection of cultural works and artifacts creates the foundation for much of the subsequent history of art. Lectures that cover the museum's important Asian, ancient Near Eastern, African, Oceanic, and pre-Hispanic collections are designed to help visitors emerge from the museum with a sense of the historical range and aesthetic qualities of these disparate but influential cultures.

A series of four lectures explores The Metropolitan Museum of Art's most famous department: the Department of European Paintings. Starting with the stylistic experiments of the Renaissance and continuing through the 19th century, these lectures show how select masterpieces by history's most influential artists—including Bernini, Canaletto, El Greco, and Monet—fit into the larger historical framework of European culture and art.

Other departments in The Metropolitan Museum of Art are devoted to other forms of art, including sculpture, drawings and prints, photography, costumes and textiles, musical instruments, arms and armor, and decorative arts. Individual lectures take you inside period rooms and detailed galleries designed to transport visitors to a different time and place. Indeed, one sees that an unspoken goal of The Metropolitan Museum of Art is to serve as a time machine in which one can experience life as a medieval warrior, a Venetian intellectual, or a 20th-century American businesswoman without abandoning the comforts of the 21st century.

While The Metropolitan Museum of Art is a global museum, its collection of American art makes it an equally viable record of the nation's aesthetic evolution. A pair of lectures explores the museum's collections of American art from the colonial era through the fracturing period of the Civil War to the start of the 20th century. Additional lectures offer insights into American works from the 20th century (along with their European counterparts) contained in the museum's Department of 20th Century Art [Department of Modern Art].

Of course, a great museum is nothing without the donors who help supply its galleries with important works of art. Among the most important donations in The Metropolitan Museum of Art's history is that made by Robert Lehman, whose collection of Old Master drawings and Italian Renaissance paintings composes an entire wing of the museum and spans a period from 1400 to 1960. In addition to lectures devoted to highlights of the Lehman Collection, the course concludes with a lecture that covers the important role individuals play in the foundation and maturation of an institution as influential as The Metropolitan Museum of Art. Without the past and continued support of curators and donors, the museum would be an empty shell overlooking Central Park instead of what it is today: an art museum richly populated with both magnificent works of art and visitors eager for a rich cultural experience.

Lecture One
The Making of the Museum

Scope: Of the world's great universal museums, The Metropolitan Museum of Art (unofficially called "the Met") is the most wide-ranging and ambitious. Its collections are truly unparalleled in their global and millennial scope and include works from every continent and most historical civilizations and nations. The first lecture will situate the museum in the historical context of the great city of New York. New York City's geographical situation, history of tolerance, easy acceptance of outsiders, and financial power drew people from all over the world, making it the largest and richest American city by the 1850s. Using maps, historical photographs, paintings, and prints, the lecture will provide a social, cultural, and economic portrait of New York City that is essential to understanding its greatest museum. From there, the lecture will address the history of the museum, its development in and around Central Park, and its layout. The lecture will conclude with thoughts on how best to approach visiting this extraordinary museum.

Outline

I. The Metropolitan Museum of Art in Manhattan, New York, is the greatest art museum in America.

    A. It is the largest museum, it has the most wide-ranging collections, and it is the crown jewel of one of the great cities of the world.

    B. There are few museums that encompass the same millennial history of mankind more comprehensively.

        1. The museum is the only great encyclopedic museum in the world.

        2. Because Americans come from all over the world, they have a duty to collect the patrimony of the great civilizations of the world.

II. The museum came about as New York City developed into the largest and most important city in the 19th century.

A. New York was first settled by the Dutch, became an English colony, and finally became part of the United States after the Revolutionary War.

B. As a result of its phenomenal growth, its worldliness, and its role as the center for receiving the great early waves of immigrants from the middle and late 19th century to the early 1920s, New York City became a global city.

C. Shortly after the Civil War, a group of prominent New Yorkers led by financier John Jay met to discuss the creation of a great art museum.
    1. They met at the Bois de Boulogne in Paris—a place that had already established an extraordinary museum—so they could learn from the city's experience.
    2. They decided to locate their museum in what was then being considered the largest urban park in America: Central Park.

D. I want to discuss the museum in two contexts: the city of New York as it developed into the art capital of the world and the context of Central Park where the museum sits.

III. You can see changing views of New York City through paintings.

A. Robert Havell, Jr.'s *View of the Bay and City of New York from Weehawken* (1840) depicts early Manhattan as a bucolic place with no particular future.

B. Childe Hassam's *Spring Morning in the Heart of the City* (1890; reworked 1895–1899) suggests a New York alive with activity.

C. George Wesley Bellows's *Pennsylvania Station Excavation* (1907–1908) depicts the unbelievable energy and intensity of Penn Station's construction.

D. Unlike Samuel Halpert and *The Flatiron Building* (1919), not all artists thought that New York City pulsed with energy. In *The City* (1927), Edward Hopper had an idea that the city was full of buildings but not humanity.

E. George Copeland Ault's *From Brooklyn Heights* (1925) depicts a melee of machines in a city that was not even imaginable to an artist like Havell, Jr.

F. John Marin's *Lower Manhattan from the River, Number 1* (1921) reflects the city's energy of business, progress, buildings, and multitudes.

G. Florine Stettheimer's *Spring Sale at Bendel's* (1921) suggests that New York City cared little about world politics because it was busy with its own prosperity.

H. Stuart Davis's *New York Mural* (1932) places onto one large canvas all the activity and excitement of New York City.

IV. As New York City developed, one needed a place of refuge, so the state legislature permitted the city to buy 700 acres of land to develop Central Park.

    A. Calvert Vaux and Frederick Law Olmstead won the competition for developing the park.

    B. They wanted to bring the landscape of the Hudson River Valley into New York City so people could walk into a facsimile of nature.

        1. There is very little architecture in the park.

        2. There are no straight lines in the park—everything waves and curves.

        3. All of art and nature are available through two huge institutions in and on the edge of the park: The Metropolitan Museum of Art and the American Museum of Natural History.

        4. Obelisk Hill features architecture, controlled water, and natural water.

    C. Central Park was a place where social classes mixed, where hundreds of languages were spoken, and where both young and old visited.

    D. It was in this setting that artists came to paint New York City.

        1. William Glackens shows us scenes of people doing various things in the park in *The Drive, Central Park* (c. 1905), *May Day, Central Park* (c. 1905), and *Central Park, Winter* (c.1905).

        2. Maurice Prendergast, in *Central Park* (c. 1914–1915), makes the park seem like an orderly realm of linear movement— which, of course, it was not.

V. Into this setting came The Metropolitan Museum of Art, which opened its first building in the Central Park location in 1880.

    A. The museum's trustees thought of it as a place where you could go to extend your culture.

B. The first building, designed by Calvert Vaux, is a neo-Baroque building with an entrance directly off the park.

C. As Fifth Avenue grew, a second building by Richard Morris Hunt was built there as a new entrance: a grand, limestone, Classical building based on the Baths of Caracalla.

D. As New York City became richer, people gave the museum more and more things; soon, the institution became something extraordinary.

    1. Frank Waller's *Interior View of the Metropolitan Museum of Art when in Fourteenth Street* (1881) was painted before the new wing on Fifth Avenue was built, and one sees the museum as a place where the imagination can run wild.

    2. The museum has become the greatest encyclopedic art museum in America, with more than 2.5 million objects.

VI. My goal is to take you into the museum and make it something you want to go to.

  A. What I want to do is divide the museum into its constituent parts and take you into it the way that all of us walk through museums.

    1. The two great civilizations that affected the ancient Mediterranean and the Western tradition—Greco-Roman and Egyptian—are on the first floor.

    2. On the second floor are the arts of Asia—China, India, Japan, and Korea—and the arts of the ancient Near East and the Islamic world.

    3. European art is on two floors: Above the main staircase are the galleries of European paintings from the late 13th century through the 19th century; below the main staircase are the three-dimensional arts of Europe mixed with a group of period rooms.

    4. In the Postwar period, the museum added enormous wings on the sides as it acquired new aesthetic territories. On the north side are the arts of America and on the south side are the arts of Africa, Oceania, the ancient Americas, and 20th-century art.

  B. The Metropolitan Museum of Art has become a global museum through time, and my tour recognizes that essential growth.

  C. I want to talk about how and why to go to a museum.

    1. A good reason to go to a museum is to learn something and feel a connection with people from the past.

2. Splitting up when visiting with a large group makes it easier to have a relationship with objects.
3. Walk around the museum rapidly, pick out the things you want to look at, then go back and explore them in depth.
4. When you are bored, it is important to leave and take a break before returning.

Recommended Reading:

Clark. *Masterpieces of Fifty Centuries: Metropolitan Museum of Art.*

de Montebello. *Met and the New Millennium: Chronicle of the Past and a Blueprint for the Future.*

———. *The Metropolitan Museum of Art Guide Revised Edition.*

Questions to Consider:

1. The Metropolitan Museum of Art is considered to be one of the world's great universal and global art museums. Why do you agree or disagree?
2. How does the museum compare in its historical and geographical context with other museums you have visited or are familiar with?

Lecture Two
The Art of Ancient Greece and Rome

Scope: All great Western art museums are rooted in collections of works of art produced by the two greatest civilizations of the ancient Mediterranean world: Greece and Rome. These two successive civilizations are viewed as the foundation of Western civilization; the museum, since its founding, has acquired works of art— through gifts, purchases, and archaeological projects—that provide New York City with a touchstone against which to measure its own cultural and artistic achievements. Although not as large as the collections in the Louvre or British museums, the Classical collections at The Metropolitan Museum of Art are of distinguished international standard. As in all collection-based lectures, a group of masterpieces will be isolated from the rest of the collection so that the visitor is not overwhelmed. These works will be selected across the mediums of ancient art—ceramics, stone, bronze, gold, stucco—and will include the Roman painted room from Boscoreale, which will introduce the viewer to the museum's practice of acquiring authentic period environments to complement individual works of art.

Outline

I. In 1870, when the museum was founded, the United States fervently believed it was the successor to Rome as the great modern nation.

    A. Most museums in Europe and America attempted to tell stories of civilization that linked the present to the great examples of Classical art from the Greco-Roman world.

    B. In 1870, the museum acquired as its first work of art a Roman sarcophagus.

    C. When the museum opened in 1880 at the Central Park location, it had a full-scale collection of plaster casts from Roman antiquity.

    D. By 1909, when the Fifth Avenue building opened, there was a new Department of Greek and Roman Art.

    E. Every detail of the museum's architecture has its roots in Rome.

        1. The arches and pendentives of the Great Room are based on the Baths of Caracalla.

  2. Vast stone walls with extraordinary arched openings have great Classical details.

  3. The black-and-white mosaic marble pavements in the Roman courtyard are based on those in Roman houses.

 F. The collections of the Department of Greek and Roman Art are immense and arranged in a series of galleries.

 G. New Yorkers hired Luigi Palma di Cesnola as the first director; his collection of art from Cyprus formed the root of the institution.

II. I am going to take you on a tour of the galleries rooted in the analysis of specific, high-quality objects so that you can establish a touchstone against which to measure other objects.

 A. The Cycladic Islands nurtured a civilization in the third millennium B.C. which produced very enigmatic works of art.

  1. The simplicity of the marble seated harp player (c. 2800–2700 B.C.) appealed to modern artists.

  2. We think of 20th-century sculpture when we look at this object.

 B. The Mycenaean civilization produced extraordinary architecture, mural paintings, and rare objects.

  1. What one learns from the stirrup jar with octopus (c. 1200–1100 B.C.) is that the Mycenaeans were a sea-based civilization.

  2. The object, like the Cycladic harp player, has the sense of being modern.

III. Arguably the greatest part of the Department of Greek and Roman Art is its collection of Archaic Greek (8th–5th century B.C.) sculpture.

 A. The development of Greek sculpture occurred between the 7th century B.C. and the 3rd century B.C. in and around Athens.

 B. The marble statue of a kouros (youth) (c. 590–580 B.C.) is the earliest of the known monumental kouros figures and is one of the most important marble objects of a walking, purposeful individual in the museum's collection.

 C. The grave stele of a youth and a little girl (c. 530 B.C.) came to the museum at three different times: the lower part with the youth and the little girl in 1911 through the Hewitt Fund, the upper part with the sphinx in 1921 through the Rogers Fund, and the remainder in 1951.

1. This work re-creates, as a great wonder of funerary sculpture, an object that had probably once been vandalized.
2. This is one of the rare fragments of Classical Greek sculpture in any museum in the world that retains part of its original coloring (polychrome).

D. All of these sculptures were painted naturalistically, creating the sense that these sculptures were infused with life.

E. The poise and gestures of the marble grave stele of a little girl (c. 450–440 B.C.) are naturalistic rather than stiff, relating to the shape of the stone. The tenderness of the object is exacerbated by its fragmentary size.

F. One of the great areas of profusion in the museum is its collection of vases (principally Attic vases) from throughout Greece and the Greek colonies in Magna Graecia (today's southern Italy and Sicily).
1. Exekias's neck-amphora with lid (c. 540 B.C.) is an example of a black-figure vase in which the painter uses the color of the clay as a background, paints the figures in black, and paints the extraneous parts with decorations.
2. One can see in this vase loop-like forms that originate in Mycenaean art.
3. A terracotta amphora by the Andokides Painter (c. 530 B.C.) represents an extraordinary scene which has greater power because the black surrounds the figures and pushes them out at us.

G. The bronze chariot inlaid with ivory (second quarter of the 6th century B.C.) is one of the largest objects in the museum; the quality of its relief shows us how widespread were skillful Greek and Etruscan artisans.

H. The Ganymede Jewelry (c. 330–300 B.C.) is a rare collection of jewelry that was probably made for a man.

IV. The museum has a superb holding of Roman art.
A. The cubiculum from the Villa of P. Fannius Synistor (c. 40–30 B.C.) is an entire room that tells how a wealthy person in the town of Boscoreale lived in Roman times.
1. One can walk into the room and live in a realm based on set designs, architecture, and color.

    2. While Roman artists did not work with perspective, you can see a clear delineation of architectural space important in the rediscovery of Roman art in the Renaissance and Neoclassical periods.

B. Looking at the portrait statue of a boy (possibly Gaius Caesar), dated from the late 1st century B.C. to the early 1st century A.D., you realize the sheer skill of Roman bronze sculptors who derived their techniques from the Greeks and in some cases surpassed them.

    1. You can see how great this statue is when comparing it with a statue of the Emperor Trebonianus Gallus (A.D. 251–253).

    2. Roman portraiture represented real people with all their peculiarities; one of the great collections of Roman portraits is at The Metropolitan Museum of Art—the funerary altar of Cominia Tyche (c. A.D. 90–100).

C. A marble sarcophagus depicting the Triumph of Dionysos and the Seasons (c. A.D. 260–270) was made for a wealthy Roman.

    1. It is the opposite of the forceful, simple Grecian funerary graves.

    2. The sarcophagus is made of Phrygian marble imported from Greece.

    3. If the Greek sculpture of death is puritanical in its reduction, this is a sculpture of almost proto-Baroque excess.

Recommended Reading:

Mertens. *Greece and Rome.*

Picón and De Puma. *Art of the Classical World in the Metropolitan Museum of Art: Greece, Cyprus, Etruria, and Rome.*

Von Bothmer. *The Metropolitan Museum of Art Guide to the Collections: Greek and Roman Art.*

Questions to Consider:

1. Choose an object from the museum's Greco-Roman collection and describe its significance to the history of Western art.

2. Ancient Greek and Roman cultures are considered to be the foundations of Western civilization. How do you see this reflected in the art presented at the museum?

Lecture Three
Ancient Egyptian Art

Scope: If Greece and Rome are the familiar civilizations of antiquity, both of them are based largely on the example of the even more ancient civilization of Egypt. With its divine pharaohs, cult of death, massive stone cities and temple-tomb complexes, highly stratified society, and polytheistic religion, the civilization of ancient Egypt survived for more than three millennia and produced millions of objects that are scattered throughout the world's museums. After its founding in 1906 with a modest collection, the museum's Department of Egyptian Art has grown into one of the largest and finest departments in America, with nearly all of its 36,000 works on public view in a major suite of galleries located directly opposite those for Greco-Roman art. The collections range from Predynastic objects to the later art of Coptic Christian culture; the objects range from constructed environments (both interior and exterior) to tiny works of gold, glass, and ceramic. The museum also has a particularly rich collection of what might be called "the art of the afterlife": mummy cases in all stages, tomb sculptures, and ritual objects.

Outline

I. While there is a whole suite of galleries devoted to the arts of ancient Greece and Rome, the museum has an equally large suite of galleries devoted to an even larger collection: the art of ancient Egypt.

   A. The Metropolitan Museum of Art was one of the early American art museums to embrace Egyptian art.

   1. In 1906, J. P. Morgan founded the Department of Egyptian Art and began to finance large archaeological investigations in Egypt.

   2. The Department of Egyptian Art is one of the largest in America and consists of more than 36,000 objects—more objects than most American museums have in their entirety.

   B. In the museum's entrance hall you are confronted with a preserved sphinx representing Hatshepsut, the only Egyptian woman who was a true pharaoh.

C. The ancient Egyptian art galleries are arranged in chronological order and by medium.

II. The galleries and displays are of extraordinary high quality.

   A. There are huge cases with many objects, including painted limestone reliefs from the Old Kingdom, rooms with reconstructions of Egyptian wall paintings, and rooms filled with pottery shards.

   B. The museum has a few rare works of art that are Predynastic (before the succession of pharaohs who came to be known as the First Dynasty), including a comb (c. 3200 B.C.) with marvelous rows of animals that create a sense of the great world open to us.

   C. Dynastic Egypt represents the world of the pyramids and the Old Kingdom, in which a pharaoh and his wife and children dominated society.

      1. Statue of Memi and Sabu (c. 2575–2465 B.C.) is a limestone portrait.

      2. Because of the relationship between writing and art, there is a good deal of knowledge about these early portraits of human beings, not all of whom were pharaohs.

      3. What is great about the museum's collection is that you can make comparisons among many objects of each type.

   D. Sphinxes were common in Egyptian art.

      1. Sphinxes like the Sphinx of Senwosret III (c. 1878–1841 B.C.) offer a sense of suppressed power.

      2. Most Egyptian objects were not made of marble because there was no marble in Egypt.

III. One of the most fascinating things about Egyptian art is that it does not change very much over 3,000 years.

   A. The stylistic qualities of form—blocky figures, thinly incised detail, polished surfaces, a quiet solidity—persist over time in such a way that it matters more how the object participated in a long tradition.

   B. Fragmentary Head of a Queen (c. 1352–1336 B.C.) is made of yellow jasper and exists in the space of the museum as a miraculously beautiful fragment.

    C. One of the great phases in the history of Egypt was that in which Amenhotep IV (Akhenaten) denounced the gods and goddesses of Egyptian art and brought monotheism to Egypt.

        1. The museum has a relief sculpture that represents the ruler sacrificing a duck (1353–1336 B.C.).

        2. Relief sculptures are made when a sculptor takes a flattened piece of limestone and cuts the figures into the stone; the figures are then rounded from within so that the ground (what should recede) is instead the foremost part.

    D. In Magical Stela (360–343 B.C.), one can see the cultural gulf between ancient Egypt and Greece.

    E. The stone objects of Egyptian art reflect the longest monolithic artistic tradition in the world because most of the stones carved as sculpture in Egypt had to be carved a certain way.

    F. There is a tradition of wooden sculpture in Egypt; unlike wooden sculpture in the rest of the world, Egyptian wood sculpture survives because the climate is so dry.

        1. The Model of a Riverboat (c. 1985 B.C.) reflects Egyptian technology, dress, and society.

        2. You can walk through the galleries and see a suite of wooden figures, like Ritual Figure (c. 1929–1878 B.C.), which have more movement and life than stone figures.

        3. One thinks back to the early kouros sculptures in the Greek galleries and realizes that the Egyptians did many things more than a millennia before the Greeks.

    G. The museum has lots of mummies, including the Coffin of Khnum-nakht (c. 1900–1800 B.C.) and the Outer Coffin of Henettawy (c. 1040–991 B.C.), both of which are divinized portraits of particular people.

IV. From the 36,000 objects in the museum's collection, I have chosen a few to give you a sense of the qualities of objects produced for the pharaoh and the courts of ancient Egypt.

    A. The Heart Scarab of Hatnofer (c. 1466 B.C.), in its simplicity and clarity, reminds one of Art Nouveau works.

    B. The Chair of Renyseneb (c. 1450 B.C.) is one of the earliest surviving chairs in the history of art.

    C. The museum also has marvelous holdings of small-scale ceramics, including a faience Sphinx of Amenhotep III (c. 1391–1353 B.C.).

D. You can get a much better idea of how ancient Egyptians lived than ancient Romans or Greeks because the Egyptian collections are largely archaeological and cover a wide range of mediums and subjects, like the bronze statue of a cat titled *Cat* (330–30 B.C.).

V. As an institution far from the origins of these cultures, The Metropolitan Museum of Art tries to give us a sense of what life and spaces were like for these cultures, which is hard to get from portable objects.

A. The Tomb of Perneb (c. 2350–2323 B.C.) was taken stone by stone from Egypt, brought to the museum, and re-created.

B. The Temple of Dendur (c. 15 B.C.) is the only Egyptian temple in its entirety which has been transported from Egypt to the United States. Its style is not much different from the style of the Tomb of Perneb.

Recommended Reading:

Aldred. *Temple of Dendur.*

Dorman. *The Metropolitan Museum of Art: Egypt and the Ancient Near East.*

Questions to Consider:

1. What is the influence of Egyptian civilization? How is this influence demonstrated in the works presented in this lecture?

2. Many of the objects in the Egyptian collection are everyday items. Why do you think these objects are considered "art" today?

Lecture Four
Asian Art

Scope: Though less developed and smaller than the Asian art collections at the Museum of Fine Arts in Boston and the Cleveland Museum of Art, those of The Metropolitan Museum of Art are wide-ranging, comprehensive, and part of a scholarly Department of Asian Art formed in 1915. This lecture explores select works from key Asian civilizations: Indian religious sculptures that emphasize movement; Chinese works including sculpture, ceramics, and the re-creation of a Chinese scholar's garden; and Japanese screens and prints. Taken together, the masterpieces in these collections create a physical context for any visitor to the museum, allowing one to emerge with a full sense of the historical range and aesthetic qualities of Asian art. Indeed, the chronological span of the Asian collection is the longest of any department in the museum.

Outline

I. Above the galleries devoted to ancient Egypt is a sequence of galleries devoted to the arts of Asia.

   A. The museum has three essential parts to its Department of Asian Art, each like a little museum.

   1. Nearest Fifth Avenue is a sequence of galleries devoted to the arts of India and Southeast Asia; the major gallery is oriented to the arts of China.

   2. Going toward the west are galleries devoted to the arts of Japan.

   3. Moored in the middle are galleries devoted to the arts of Korea.

   B. The Department of Asian Art has fewer objects than the Department of Egyptian Art, but its objects are more varied.

   C. The department was started after the departments of Greco-Roman art and Egyptian art. Its galleries are much harder to get to in the museum and almost require a separate visit if one wants to successfully view them.

D. The collections unfortunately are not the greatest collections of Asian art in America; that honor goes to the Museum of Fine Arts in Boston.

E. Though the Korean gallery is beautifully installed, I am going to concentrate on the older, more continuous civilizations to give you a sense of the richness and variety of the collections.

II. India was the civilization nearest to the West and the only part of Asia that encountered at an early date the civilizations of ancient Greece.

    A. There was a fascination in the objects left in the wake of Alexander the Great's conquests (which extended into modern-day India).

    B. The beginning of trade relationships between far-western India and parts of Europe reflects a leakage of Asian and European culture.

    C. The Standing Bodhisattva Maitreya (c. 3rd century) suggests early Indian sculptors' knowledge of Greek traditions.
        1. The sculpture reflects Hellenistic sculpture in its fascination with the rhythms of drapery.
        2. The grey schist used in this sculpture embodies the Classical form.

    D. Shiva as Lord of Dance (Nataraja) (c. 11th century) is a sculpture that almost everyone knows from reproductions and associates with India.
        1. The Hindu god is balanced with a clarity and strength of form that is extraordinary when you consider it was cast in bronze.
        2. One has to think about this sculpture as not merely a representation of a dance but as a *tour de force* of bronze illusionism—the control of heavy material in bringing together perfect balance.
        3. This is an early piece from the Chola dynasty, probably the greatest early master dynasty of bronze sculpture; Chola bronzes are among the pinnacles of Indian art.

    E. The sculpture of a loving couple (Mithuna) from the 13th century is made from ferruginous stone, which is easy to carve after quarrying but becomes harder as it rests in the atmosphere.
        1. Ferruginous stone is prized by sculptors in particular regions of India.
        2. Works like this were taken from larger buildings; its particular rhythms rhyme with those of other figures.

3. Unlike the inertness of Egyptian sculpture, one feels these are real figures that can move.
4. This is an example of a type of Indian sculpture that is very important on the temples that remain in India.

F. Yashoda and Krishna (c. early 14th century) depict something we have not seen in any of the cultures we have examined so far: the bond between a mother and a child.
1. We see a god and a human together, much like the Virgin and Christ Child.
2. The sculpture can be compared to the museum's many images from the history of Christian art that deal with the relationship between the divine child and the human mother.

III. The museum's collections of art from China is much larger than its Indian collections, and are definitive collections in which you can understand the whole history of Chinese art.

A. A set of early Chinese bronze ritual vessels (rare in American museums) were perhaps used for a burial.
1. They were all found together in one tomb or in a Chinese collection in 1901 and sold to the museum in 1924.
2. The forms overlap each other in complex patterns.
3. In China, bronze casting was early on at a very high level.

B. The Altarpiece Dedicated to Buddha Maitreya (A.D. 524) is extraordinary because it is inscribed and dated, something very rare in early Asian art. As in this altarpiece, many Christian altarpieces reflect a deified figure in the center flanked by other figures.

C. The Seated Buddha (c. A.D. 650) is almost weightless because it is made from dried lacquer; this lightness is inherent both to its physical and aesthetic properties.

D. *Summer Mountains* (11th century), attributed to Qu Ding, is a huge painting that can be explored with a leisure its length permits.

E. Chinese ceramics are one of the great glories of world ceramics, and the museum has a very large and important collection that includes a jar (1426–1435) from the Ming dynasty. These were the kinds of ceramics collected in the West, where porcelain was redeveloped in the 17th and 18th centuries using Asian models.

F. Chuba's cut velvet from the 17th century is one of the best-preserved pieces of textile in the museum.

G. The Chinese collection revolves around the Astor Court: a re-creation of a scholar's garden in China that one can move through in a manner similar to the Temple of Dendur or the Roman cubiculum.

IV. We end with a few objects from the great cultures of Japan.

    A. The earliest is the clay bust of a warrior (5th–6th century) reminiscent of western Mexican ceramics and possessing an animistic force.

    B. Wisdom King Fudö (12th century) was made to be worshipped as a pair of guardians on either side of a historic Buddha.

    C. The Battles of the Hôgen and Heiji (17th century) are a pair of screens that represent these historic Japanese battles in such a way that one can spend hours looking at them.

    D. Ogata Körin's *Rough Waves* (c. 1704–1709) is a two-fold screen in which the energy of the water, without a point of reference, creates a terrifying pictorial world that is made palatable by being so simple.

    E. Katsushika Hokusai's *The Great Wave at Kanagawa* (c. 1830–1832) is part of a series of prints depicting views of Mt. Fuji.

        1. The vast wave (with its decorative froths) indicates that Hokusai knew about Körin's painting.

        2. The print was given to the museum by the Havemeyer family, who received their instruction in art from people like Claude Monet, Mary Cassatt, and Edgar Degas.

Recommended Reading:

Barnhart. *Asia (The Metropolitan Museum of Art Series).*

Valenstein. *Handbook of Chinese Ceramics.*

Questions to Consider:

1. Many cultures are represented in the Asian galleries at the museum. Which portion of the collection speaks to you the most and why?

2. Some areas of the Asian galleries may represent cultures unfamiliar to some visitors. What art object presented in this session was a surprising or new discovery for you and why?

Lecture Five
The Ancient Near East and Islamic Art

Scope: Housed in two separate departments with adjacent suites of galleries, works of art produced in what we now call the Middle East have been an essential part of The Metropolitan Museum of Art's presentation of world art since the 1890s. The Department of Ancient Near Eastern Art includes works from the various civilizations that appeared in the Tigris and Euphrates valleys during the 4th millennium B.C. and subsequently spread in all directions. Visitors will see works of art that vary from the earliest Bronze Age objects made from primitive alloys to entire segments of urban palaces. The collections are vast enough to show the early mastery of glass, ceramic, stone carving, bronze, and single-mineral metallurgy in various successive urban cultures. These various cultures were succeeded by a politically diverse group of Muslims who collectively controlled territories that spanned from southern Portugal to what is now Bangladesh—an area larger than the Roman Empire. The Islamic collections of the museum are among the largest and most important on public display in any museum in the world, and this lecture will feature a select group of ceramics, textiles, and Islamic texts whose geographic origins span the area controlled by Islam during the Middle Ages.

Outline

I. The arts of the Middle East—the parts of art history that are the least represented in most American museums—are divided between two departments at The Metropolitan Museum of Art.

   A. Middle Eastern civilization began just as early as Egyptian civilization. It became more varied and complex with the conversion of almost that entire part of the world to Islam in the 1st millennium A.D.

   B. The museum received objects of ancient Near Eastern art early in its history, but it was not until 1956 that it created a Department of Ancient Near Eastern Art to give a full picture of the region's various civilizations.

C. The department is located above the Department of Greek and Roman Art. In back is a large suite of galleries reserved for the arts of Islam from its beginning to recent times.

II. This lecture will comprise one cultural area over millennia of time, and it will deal with the importance of Islam for the arts and the radical transformation of the arts under Islam in the ancient Middle East.

    A. The storage jar decorated with mountain goats (4th millennium B.C.) relates to the Mycenaean jar with the octopus design.

        1. The longer one looks at this jar, the more one becomes interested in its forms, and the more it becomes a work of art.

        2. One sees in this jar a remarkable sense of design that will impact succeeding generations.

    B. The kneeling bull holding a spouted vessel (3100–2900 B.C.) is an object of high metropolitan culture.

        1. It is pure silver, which indicates that people by this time were sophisticated miners working at a sophisticated level.

        2. It is an object of new sensibility from a new civilization.

    C. The headdress, necklace, and hair ribbons (2600–2500 B.C.) were made in the ancient city of Ur. Modern scholars think they gave a sparkling leafiness to a ruler as he or she moved.

    D. The head of a ruler (2300–2000 B.C.), made of arsenic-induced copper, is hollow and is among the earliest cast bronzes or proto-bronzes in the history of art. It is one of the earliest portraits with a force of realism and reflects much of Roman portraiture from two millennia later; it is also more observed than the portraits in the Egyptian galleries.

III. The cities that these men ruled were extraordinary. Unfortunately, in the United States the collection of archaeological material from these cities is very poor; John D. Rockefeller, however, managed to secure a few rare, large-scale archaeological pieces.

    A. Relief panels (883–859 B.C.) from the city of Nimrud are made from Mosul marble (a kind of alabaster).

        1. The figures look more like Egyptian art because they are carved from a similar hard stone that the Egyptians used.

        2. The figures give us an idea of the city's scale.

    B. Two panels with striding lions (604–562 B.C.) were made during the historical realm of Nebuchadnezzar II (r. 604–562 B.C.).

1. The glazes of brilliant green, yellow, blue, and white form a chromatic world that the sun would have enhanced.
2. The monumental dimensions and chromatic intensity of the panels are unknown in the history of art.

C. Metallurgy was an extraordinary part of these civilizations, as seen in the vessel terminating in the forepart of a fantastic leonine creature (5th century B.C.).

D. The ewer with dancing females (6th–7th century), like a good deal of the museum's metallurgy, came rather recently to the museum as the department has become more acquisitive in this area of art history.
1. Its perfection of form links it to Greco-Roman works.
2. The ewer is a bridge to Islamic art because it was made not too long before another ewer (7th century) in which there is little representational function.
3. Islamic art had no representational function but was abstract and based on plant life and patterns (to avoid images that could be worshipped).

IV. The museum has one of the great Islamic collections of a general art museum in the world.

A. The Department of Islamic Art was founded in 1963 but became a large department and reinstalled itself in glorious galleries in the 1970s.

B. A bowl from the 10th century B.C. possesses nothing that can be worshipped. The text around the rim reflects a protection of form, meaning, and content.

C. The plaque (10th–early 11th century B.C.) is a tiny object made of ivory. Because it is repetitive, it was probably part of a piece of furniture (similar to the Egyptian chair with its little pieces of ivory).

D. One of the most glorious objects is the mihrab (A.D. 1354–1355/A.H. 755), which is a prayer opening.
1. This is a purely Islamic form devoid of representation, with only abstract patterns and three levels of text.
2. Mathematicians and fractal geometers have studied its patterns and forms.

E. The niche design carpet (late 16th century) is a prayer carpet; its colors have survived and are in a wonderful state.

F. The museum has a wonderful collection of Islamic texts that—when related to those in the Morgan Library, the New York Public Library, and the Hispanic Society—is part of the great collections of Islamic texts in the world.

    1. The Qur'an manuscript (13th–14th century) from Spain is pure ornamentation.

    2. The illustrations in *Shahnama* (*The Book of Kings*) *of Shah Tahmasp* (c. 1520–1522) are an exception to this iconoclasm. The quality of the illustration, the quality of the paper, and the placement on the page mean that this book is one of the pinnacles of illustrated books in any culture.

    3. *Tughra* of Sultan Sulaiman the Magnificent (16th century) is the easiest piece of calligraphy to understand in the museum; a signature done in a decorative calligraphy that suggests the meaning of the Sultan's name.

G. The entire idea of The Metropolitan Museum of Art is that we are all time travelers learning about civilizations other than our own, an idea reflected in the Nur al-Din Room (1707/A.H. 1119).

Recommended Reading:

Muscarella. *Bronze and Iron: Ancient Near Eastern Artifacts in the Metropolitan Museum of Art.*

Pittman. *Art of the Bronze Age: Southeastern Iran, Western Central Asia, and the Indus Valley.*

Welch. *The Islamic World.*

Questions to Consider:

1. Choose an object in the museum's collection of Near Eastern art and explain why it appeals to you.

2. Do you believe that objects used in worship and religious devotion are worthy of display in an art museum? Why or why not?

Lecture Six

European Painting I—The Renaissance

Scope: There is no doubt that, despite the wide range of its collections, the most famous and best known department at The Metropolitan Museum of Art is the Department of European Paintings. With painted masterpieces ranging from the 14th through 19th centuries, the collections rival those of any of the great European museums. Because of the scale and definitive ambitions of this collection, I will devote four separate lectures to its treasures. The collection of 14th and 15th century paintings, divided between the Department of Medieval Art and the Department of European Paintings, is particularly strong in masterpieces of both Italian and Flemish art. This lecture will deal with the birth of figural illusionism in northern Italy in the 14th century and the subsequent development of devices that create the illusion of deep pictorial space. The lecture will also stress the separate but interdependent traditions of Renaissance painting in Italy and Flanders in the 15th century, paying particular attention to the development of portraiture and the technical innovation of oil painting in the north. The lecture will culminate with two works by Sandro Botticelli and Piero di Cosimo that show how ambitious a period the Renaissance was in the history of art.

Outline

I. The works of art that almost everybody wants to see at The Metropolitan Museum of Art are the collections of European paintings from the Renaissance to the 19th century.

   A. A sequence of rooms at the top of the vast staircase is devoted to the museum's collection of European painting.

   B. The Department of European Paintings is one of the greatest in the world and is so large and important that I am devoting four lectures to it rather than one.

II. Let us begin our tour at the chronological beginning of the installation with the arts in the early Renaissance and late Gothic period in Italy, in which the arts really came together.

A. During the 13th and 14th centuries, Italian paintings went from being flat to being illusionist by giving volume to figures.

B. In Berlinghiero's *Madonna and Child* (c. 1230), there is no psychological relationship between the two figures. They are seated in front of a flat, gilded background with no hint of pictorial space.

C. In Duccio di Buoninsegna's *Madonna and Child* (c. 1300), the whole act of looking is an act of intimacy.
    1. There is a deep psychological relationship between the child and the mother.
    2. The child has the quality of an actual infant, despite its odd proportions.
    3. The conquest of space through shading, overlapping, and gesture creates something new in Italian art around 1300.

D. What one sees in Giotto di Bondone's *The Epiphany* (possibly c. 1320) is that the picture offers a sense of plausible pictorial space.

E. We can see gradually the birth of pictorial space as we go through the galleries.

III. When we are looking at pictures like these on the walls of the museum, we are looking oftentimes at fragments of earlier works of art that were much larger and more complex.

A. The subject of Simone Martini's *Saint Andrew* (probably c. 1326) looks out of the picture, meaning that he is a fragment of an altarpiece in which several saints were probably looking at a central figure of Christ.
    1. Despite this, the figure has volume like Giotto's figures.
    2. The work recalls Gothic painting.

B. Sassetta's *The Journey of the Magi* (c. 1435) is another fragment.
    1. It was cut from an altarpiece scene of the Magi visiting the Virgin Mary: *Adoration of the Magi* (c. 1435).
    2. One has to think carefully in looking at a work of art, especially when analyzing its composition.
    3. The museum displays this painting without a frame, so one can see the original edges of the painting.

IV. There were equal innovations in the history of art in the 14th and 15th centuries to the north of Europe, particularly in Flanders.

- **A.** I want to compare a major Italian painting of the Crucifixion and a major northern painting of the same subject to show how different were the two systems.
- **B.** In *The Crucifixion* (c. 1420), attributed to Fra Angelico, one sees a wonderful sense of volume. The work is painted with tempera, in which pigments were suspended in egg white, producing a matte surface that looked like gouache or a water-based paint.
- **C.** Jan van Eyck and the group of artists around him in Bruges and Ghent began to suspend pigment in oil, creating the kind of oil painting we know today.
- **D.** In Van Eyck's *The Crucifixion; The Last Judgment* (c. 1430), one sees the Crucifixion on the left and the Last Judgment on the right, with the two panels forming an altarpiece rather than a diptych. The scene seems to be set in the here and now rather than in a mythical place like Fra Angelico's painting.

V. Virtually every important town in Italy produced its own school of paintings; unfortunately, in the United States our collections are not large enough that we can devote an entire gallery to a single school.

- **A.** Andrea Mantegna's *The Adoration of the Shepherds* (shortly after 1450) is a radical advance in pictorial space. One sees that the native of Ferrara already knew the lessons of one-point perspective that had been developed by architects and painters in Florence.
- **B.** The 15th century is the first century in which artists sign their works in profusion and have a sense of their own identity and their potential as major artists.
- **C.** Carlo Crivelli's *Pietà* (1476) possesses a remarkable emotional intensity that reflects the individual characteristics of the regional schools in Italy.
- **D.** A series of portraits illustrates how much the individual painter and the subject of his painting transformed during the Renaissance.
    1. Fra Filippo Lippi's *Portrait of a Woman with a Man at a Casement* (c. 1440) depicts a woman in strict profile, like a Roman coin.
    2. *Portrait of a Carthusian* (1446) by Petrus Christus is a tiny, detailed painting you feel you could hold in your hands.
    3. Rogier van der Weyden's *Francesco d'Este (born around 1430, died after 1475)* from around 1460 possesses a realism that reminds one of portraits from Rome and other cultures in

which the force of the character is so strong that we feel we are looking at an actual person.

4. Hans Memling's *Tommaso di Folco Portinari (1428–1501)* and *Maria Portinari (Maria Maddalena Baroncelli, born 1456)*, both from around 1470, are portraits with a religious function, but they also tell us what a particular individual looked like in the 15th century.

E. Another northern/southern comparison can be made between two works depicting the Virgin Mary and the Christ Child.

1. *Virgin and Child* (c. 1455–1460) by Dieric Bouts invests the Virgin and the Christ Child with a kind of humanity unprecedented in the earlier history of art.

2. *Madonna and Child* (probably late 1480s) by Giovanni Bellini displays a strong interest in Classicism; if we walked into the Greco-Roman galleries, we would find figures like this baby.

F. Two large panel pictures by two Italian artists make one aware that paintings were not always easel pictures or altarpieces.

1. Sandro Botticelli's *Three Miracles of Saint Zenobius* (1500–1510), completed almost a century after the development of one-point perspective, commands a new, total pictorial space and has a sense of being part of a decorative scheme that brings religion into the secular realm.

2. Piero di Cosimo's *A Hunting Scene* lacks the precision and sense of order that is so important in Botticelli's painting; its disordered landscape reflects the troubling quality of humankind.

3. We can see in these two paintings that the Renaissance was not always clear, was not always religious, did not have a single meaning, and was an ambitious time in the history of art.

Recommended Reading:

Hartt. *The Metropolitan Museum of Art: Renaissance in Italy and Spain.*

Snyder. *The Renaissance in the North.*

Questions to Consider:

1. Describe the advances in the portrayal of figural illusionism in the museum's paintings from the early Renaissance.

2. Describe the pictorial dialogue between the Renaissance artists of Italy and Flanders. What are the similarities and differences in their respective styles and techniques?

Lecture Seven
European Painting II—16ᵗʰ–17ᵗʰ Centuries

Scope: Although The Metropolitan Museum of Art possesses no paintings by Leonardo da Vinci or Michelangelo, it does have a masterpiece by Raphael. From this superb altarpiece flows an almost unbelievable group of works by virtually every master of painting in Italy, Germany, Spain, France, Flanders, and Holland—all of which are arranged chronologically and culturally in galleries that separate the masters either by region (in Italy) or by nation (the rest of Europe). This lecture moves forward into the 16ᵗʰ and 17ᵗʰ centuries and deals with the extraordinary profusion of painting in Europe during the period known as the High Renaissance. This lecture will analyze major works by the most important artists of the period: Dürer, Holbein the Younger, Bronzino, Titian, Caravaggio, Bruegel the Elder, El Greco, Velázquez, Rubens, Poussin, Rembrandt, ter Brugghen, Vermeer, and van Ruisdael. These artists and their works will be placed in the larger context of European cultural history.

Outline

I.   This lecture moves forward into the 16ᵗʰ and 17ᵗʰ centuries and deals with the extraordinary profusion of painting in Europe during the High Renaissance.

   A. This period is dominated by three great artists: Michelangelo, Leonardo da Vinci, and Raphael.

   B. While the museum has only drawings by Michelangelo and da Vinci, it does have one of the greatest paintings outside of Europe by Raphael.

   1. *Madonna and Child Enthroned with Saints* (c. 1504) is an altarpiece so large that one has to stand back in order to get a sense of its grandeur and space; no gallery in the museum is as large as the space for which this work was originally painted.

   2. The altarpiece depicts a sense of ecclesiastical time, more clear in the lunette depicting God flanked by two gorgeous angels.

       3.   There is a maturity in the work that is more in the history of the style of Renaissance painting than in the age of the artist himself.

   C.   An artist equally great in northern painting as Raphael was in southern painting was Albrecht Dürer.

       1.   One gets a sense of Protestantism in *Virgin and Child with Saint Anne* (probably 1519), which presents the Virgin not as a queen to worship but as a homely young girl.

       2.   One sees a complex, triangular relationship that reflects intimate family ties, as if what is written in the Bible is about real human beings.

   D.   One contrasts Dürer with Hans Holbein the Younger, another German artist who worked in the area between what is now Switzerland, Germany, and France.

       1.   The subject of Holbein's *Portrait of a Member of the Wedigh Family, Probably Hermann Wedigh (died 1560)* (1532) knows he is being represented and looks back at the viewer with an accepting glance.

       2.   The artist reflects the beginning of internationalism in art.

   E.   We will see a lot of border crossings in this lecture as artists move from one nation and one school to another.

II. A sequence of three Italian paintings made in response to the perfection of Raphael's painting reflect different strategies for the possibilities of painting after it attains this kind of perfection.

   A.   The first of these works is *Portrait of a Young Man* (1530s) by Bronzino.

       1.   One sees a level of pictorial perfection greater than Raphael and turned not toward the sacred but the secular.

       2.   The subject turns his head, body, and eyes in an example of Mannerism—art that is about art itself and in which all artifice is turned toward the humblest of subjects.

   B.   Titian's *Venus and the Lute Player* (c. 1565–1570) has none of Bronzino's perfection of form and smoothness of surface.

       1.   The work is painted very roughly; one can see the texture of the canvas.

       2.   Titian was interested in the conveyance of light and in the painter's own gesture; he wanted the viewer to see the picture as something made by hand instead of something so perfect that one cannot imagine a hand touching it.

- **C.** The third avenue for painting after Raphael can be seen in Caravaggio's *The Musicians* (c. 1595).
  - **1.** Though its surface is beautifully calm, the painting is much thicker and can be compared to a Botticelli, Bronzino, or Raphael.
  - **2.** Caravaggio was the artist with the greatest international effect.

III. A series of artists who crossed boundaries were about the general European nature of art rather than about a specific country.

- **A.** We look first at *The Harvesters* (1565) by Pieter Bruegel the Elder.
  - **1.** One sees a pure landscape without biblical or literary allusions.
  - **2.** This painting is about a particular time of year in central Europe and is one of a sequence of paintings split up through time.

- **B.** El Greco's *View of Toledo* (c. 1597–1599) is a more troubling landscape and the only landscape in his career. It is one of the great works of Spanish art and was made by a man of Greek origins who learned Italian and spent the rest of his life in Spain.

- **C.** Diego Velázquez was probably the greatest Spanish painter of the 17th century.
  - **1.** When he was in Rome, he painted *Juan de Pareja (born about 1610, died 1670)* in 1650, which conveys the figure's life with simple strokes of paint.
  - **2.** He takes the gestures of Titian and the painters of Venice and turns them onto a humble servant.

- **D.** Peter Paul Rubens was an artist born in Flanders who made his early career in Italy.
  - **1.** The museum has many of his paintings, but the finest is Rubens, *His Wife Helena Fourment (1614–1673), and Their Son Peter Paul (born 1637)* from around the late 1630s.
  - **2.** The painting tells us that a man of humble birth could die one of the wealthiest and most respected men in all of Europe.

- **E.** Nicolas Poussin was a French artist who spent the rest of his life in Rome. *The Abduction of the Sabine Women* (probably 1633–1634) recalls the Badminton sarcophagus with its riotous figures in relief.

IV. We end the lecture in Holland, which was dominated by Rembrandt van Rijn.

    A. The museum has a great collection of Rembrandts: works from his circle, works that are now attributed to someone else, and works that everyone accepts as Rembrandts.

    B. The undeniable masterpiece of the museum's Rembrandt collection is *Aristotle with a Bust of Homer* (1653).

        1. Rembrandt dresses Aristotle as if he were an Orientalist figure looking at a proper Classical bust, indicating a transference of knowledge from one generation to another.

        2. Like Titian's painting, this work is rough and possesses an extraordinary depth of blackness; figures emerge from the darkness of the picture as if emerging into light.

    C. Not all Dutch artists were Protestants; Hendrick ter Brugghen was a closet Catholic. Because Catholic worship was forbidden in Dutch cities, no one would have seen *The Crucifixion with the Virgin and Saint John* (c. 1625) except for a fervent worshipper.

    D. Holland's other well-known painter was Johannes (Jan) Vermeer, whose pictures were rediscovered in the 19th century.

        1. The museum has five paintings by Vermeer.

        2. *Allegory of the Catholic Faith* (c. 1670) does not look like other Vermeers.

        3. All of the allegories of religion (a crucifixion, a cup for communion, a snake, an apple) are present in this picture.

        4. The tapestry pulled aside suggests that Vermeer was Catholic.

    E. The jollity of the Dutch is reflected in Frans Hals's *Young Man and Woman in an Inn* (*"Yonker Ramp and His Sweetheart"*) from 1623; it is as if the painting is itself boisterous rather than representing boisterousness.

    F. Jacob Isaacksz van Ruisdael's *Wheat Fields* (c. 1670) is one of the most beautiful paintings in the museum. It is a deeply Protestant picture that does not require a divine image or a saint in order for one to understand the beauty and divinity of the world.

Recommended Reading:

Quodbach. *The Age of Rembrandt: Dutch Paintings in The Metropolitan Museum of Art.*

Rousseau. *Guide to the Picture Galleries.*

©2008 The Teaching Company.

Questions to Consider:

1. The museum is considered to be one of the great universal and global art museums in the world. Why do you agree or disagree?

2. The museum is fortunate to own three paintings by Vermeer. What is so unique about Vermeer's style and approach to painting that makes him so revered?

Lecture Eight
European Painting III—18th Century

Scope: Although there is not a pronounced break in style between the 17th and 18th centuries in European painting, the sheer volume and quality of the collection at The Metropolitan Museum of Art prompts the need for an entire lecture devoted to the 18th century, which culminated politically with the French Revolution of 1789. The collection contains a superb group of Venetian and Roman 18th-century paintings by Ricci, Giovanni Battista and Giovanni Domenico Tiepolo, Canaletto, and Guardi; an important collection of French Rococo painting by Watteau, Chardin, Boucher, Greuze, Fragonard, and David (whose *The Death of Socrates* ties a scene from ancient history with the artist's contemporary political reality); and a major group of British Grand Tour portraits by Reynolds, Gainsborough, and Lawrence. The lecture will culminate in an analysis of Goya's sad and tragic *Manuel Osorio Manrique de Zuñiga (1784–1792)* from around the 1790s.

Outline

I. The largest paintings in the museum's collection are from the 18th century.

    A. One enters the museum's collection toward the end of the narrative of European paintings told in the museum's galleries.

    B. Most European cities in the 18th century were easily accessible by water or coach, and cosmopolitan travel developed.

        1. Gentlemen and ladies of certain social orders made grand tours to other countries to learn and visit important people.

        2. There was also a sense of the shrinking of Europe, which created a high level of painting.

    C. The only country that saw a decline in art production was Holland.

    D. England, France, Italy, and Spain saw an abundance of talent, and that is the talent I will focus on in this lecture.

II. The city of Venice produced more great artists than Rome; its artists have always appealed to American collectors.

A. The museum has the best sketch for Sebastiano Ricci's *The Baptism of Christ* (c. early 18th century).
 1. The sketch is not only for the painting but for the surrounding faux architecture and sculpture.
 2. Held above Christ is a fluttering robe and a cast of hundreds who move in a wonderful sense associated with the motion of late-Baroque or early-Rococo art.

B. The sense of captured motion is an achievement of 17th-century Baroque painting, and it intensified during the 18th century.

C. Giovanni Battista Tiepolo was the greatest fresco painter/decorator in Venice after Ricci (and in many ways surpassed him).
 1. *The Triumph of Marius* (1729) is almost 20 feet tall and was part of a series of heroic decorations celebrating the pageantry of history.
 2. *Allegory of the Planets and Continents* (1752) is a cartoon for one of the largest frescoes he ever painted, *Apollo and the Four Continents* (1753), located in Germany.
 3. The sketch was given to the museum by Mrs. Charles Wrightsman, one of the most important donors of the post-World War II period of the museum's history.

D. Tiepolo's son, Giovanni Domenico Tiepolo, painted *A Dance in the Country* (c. 1755). The work represents a group of *Commedia dell'arte* figures; its quality of joy and simplicity of movement create a sense that the pictorial world is less static than the real world.

E. Today, the most famous Venetian painters of the 18th century are the view painters. Of these, the most famous is Canaletto, whose *Piazza San Marco* (possibly late 1720s) conveys, with a kind of joy and life, a tourist site that was visited as much by foreigners as by Italians.

F. Whereas Canaletto's paintings are precise, in Francesco Guardi's *Fantastic Landscape* (probably 1760s) everything moves.

III. The country that was the most important in terms of art production in the 18th century was France.

 A. France played a rather small role in the 17th century, but in the 18th century it had many great painters.
  1. Paris soon supplanted Rome as the most important city for the arts in Europe.

    2. The city had a concentration of artists and art-world people that is very much like New York City today.

B. Jean-Antoine Watteau, unlike Rubens, painted tiny paintings. He borrowed figures from the *Commedia dell'arte*, but for him they became melancholic figures, such as in *Mezzetin* (probably 1718–1720).

C. After Watteau, there are two artists who struggled against each other for dominance in Paris.
    1. Jean-Baptiste Siméon Chardin painted both exquisite still lifes and genre scenes of the bourgeoisie.
    2. One cannot read the brushstrokes in *Soap Bubbles* (c. 1734), but the work has a painterly quality that is an important part of Chardin's aesthetic.
    3. *Soap Bubbles* is also a Protestant painting in that it finds beauty in the ordinary.
    4. Chardin's chief rival was François Boucher, the favorite painter of Madame de Pompadour (the mistress of King Louis XV).
    5. In *The Toilet of Venus* (1751), one sees a goddess in comparison to Chardin's humble subjects.
    6. Boucher's painting is an example of Rococo painting, which has none of the bombast of Baroque art and is about aristocratic pleasure and the joy of sensuality in life.

D. Jean Baptiste Greuze's *Broken Eggs* (1756) combines the sensuality of Boucher's painting and the humble subject matter of Chardin to create a new morality tale.

E. Jean Honoré Fragonard was, after Boucher, the great Rococo painter of pleasure. *The Love Letter* (c. 1770) is a quickly painted essay in gold, brown, and pale green.

F. The opposite of *The Love Letter* is Jacques-Louis David's *The Death of Socrates* (1787).
    1. There is an incredible theatrical sense to this picture.
    2. It has a similar attitude to Raphael's work in terms of surface, paint, correctness, and clarity.
    3. David was involved in the French Revolution in 1789; one feels that the liberty of Socrates is being given up by the tyranny of a government.

IV. The London art world of the 18th century was rich but not as great as France. There were three artists who dominated it in the later years of the 18th century.

    A. The most important of these artists was Sir Joshua Reynolds. In *Captain George K. H. Coussmaker (1759–1801)* (1782), Reynolds used his knowledge of art history to give a puffed sense of importance to the aristocracy of important people in England.

    B. Thomas Gainsborough painted very large portraits of important people that were shown in the Royal Academy exhibitions (the equivalent of the Salon exhibitions in Paris). *Mrs. Grace Dalrymple Elliott (1754?–1823)*, from 1778, displays consummate pictorial skills—one can read every stroke of Gainsborough's brush.

    C. Sir Thomas Lawrence's *Elizabeth Farren (born about 1759, died 1829)*, from 1790, depicts one of London's most important stage actresses with a fluttering confidence and bravura that reflects Rubens's earlier portrait of his wife.

V. I end this lecture with a painting that is tender, charming, and also infinitely sad and ultimately tragic: Francisco de Goya y Lucientes's *Don Manuel Osorio Manrique de Zuñiga (1784–1792)*, made around the 1790s. The work depicts a precarious dance of death which Goya subtly shows in the shadows.

Recommended Reading:

Marandel. *Europe in the Age of Enlightenment and Revolution (The Metropolitan Museum of Art Series).*

Rousseau. *Guide to the Picture Galleries.*

Questions to Consider:

1. The museum has an excellent collection of Venetian and Roman 18th-century paintings. Choose one that is your favorite and explain its significance for yourself and within the museum's collection.

2. How is *The Death of Socrates* a political commentary? In what ways does it represent the contemporary reality of the time in which it was painted?

Lecture Nine
European Painting IV—19th Century

Scope: In 1929, when it received the gift of the collection of Horace and Louisine Havemeyer, The Metropolitan Museum of Art immediately possessed the single most important public collection in America of Modernist French painting. With masterpieces by Corot, Courbet, Manet, Degas, Monet, and Cézanne, the collection was unparalleled; since other major collections have been added to it and additional works have been purchased by the museum, the museum now has perhaps the best and most balanced collection of French painting from 1830 to 1900 in any universal art museum. This lecture will explore some of the museum's treasures by touching on the opposition between controlled artists who followed Rubens and sensual artists who followed Poussin, by studying the influence of Constable and Turner on subsequent French artists, by understanding 19th-century landscape painting as the total expression of emotion, by witnessing the controversy that began to dominate French painting, and by confronting the rise of Impressionism and Postimpressionism.

Outline

I. In 1929 the museum received the bequest of Mr. and Mrs. Horace Havemeyer, which included one of the most important collections of Impressionist and Modernist pictures. Their collection included works by Manet, Degas, Monet, and Renoir—artists who, at the time, were in very few European museums.

   A. With the death of important patrons and enormous gifts, the collections of 19th-century art outgrew the physical holdings of the Department of European Paintings.

   B. The André Meyer Wing was developed particularly for Realist, Impressionist, and Postimpressionist paintings.

   C. The collection is overwhelmingly French, but the richness of France is even greater than it was in the 18th century.

   D. Art in 18th-century France was founded on the opposition between the controlled Rubénistes and the sensual Poussinistes; this is the same case for art in 19th-century France.

1. *Joseph-Antoine Moltedo (born 1775)*, painted by Jean-Auguste-Dominique Ingres around 1810, is an early portrait with the glassy, controlled surface that reminds one of Bronzino.
2. Eugène Delacroix, the Romantic to Ingres's Classicist, painted *The Abduction of Rebecca* (1846), in which color becomes a major part of conveying the emotions in a work of art.
3. We thus have an opposition between artists of color and emotion on the one hand and rational, controlled artists on the other.

II. With this opposition in mind, we are going to take a detour and look at the work of the two greatest English artists of the 18th century who are unlike those of the last lecture.

   A. John Constable was very much admired by Delacroix and by the admirers of color and emotion. *Salisbury Cathedral from the Bishop's Grounds* (c. 1825) is fascinating in the context of New York City, particularly because it is an oil study for a finished picture which is in the Frick Collection.

   B. Constable's painting can be contrasted with Joseph Mallord William Turner's *Venice, from the Porch of the Madonna della Salute* (c. 1835).
      1. One has the sense that Turner is competing against Canaletto.
      2. There is a quality of watercolor and a transparency of atmosphere in the picture.

   C. Both Constable and Turner were admired by young French painters, and they were both artists whose careers were dedicated to painting the landscape, a subject which has not dominated the lectures so far.

III. In the 19th century, landscape painting became the greatest expression of emotions.

   A. In the late 1820s and early 1830s, a group of young artists painted together in and around the Forest of Fontainebleau, deciding it was as interesting as the countryside of Rome, which landscape painters previously had painted.

   B. The most productive and interesting of these painters was Jean-Baptiste Camille Corot. *Fontainebleau: Oak Trees at Bas-Bréau* (1832 or 1833) is painted and ordered so beautifully that we do not need allegory, religion, or history to understand it.

C. Pierre-Étienne-Théodore Rousseau threw his emotion into the representation of the Forest of Fontainebleau in his last great unfinished picture, *The Forest in Winter at Sunset* (1845–1867).

D. The last of the three landscapes by artists who come in the stead of Constable and Turner is Jean-François Millet.
   1. The museum has a painting from his series on the four seasons, *Haystacks: Autumn* (c. 1874).
   2. There is a sense of storytelling in the picture that indicates that Millet, Rousseau, and Corot painted the French landscape in completely different ways.

IV. Gustave Courbet and Édouard Manet began to dominate French painting in a way that has more to do with controversy and shock value than a respect for traditions.

A. Gustave Courbet painted the landscape of his birth in *Young Women from the Village* (1852).
   1. The landscape is alive with differences of class, intention, and belonging.
   2. The picture asks questions about politics, troubling those who thought that art should not address real concerns.
   3. Courbet's style of painting, with thick paint and a confidence in the subject matter, made him shocking.

B. Édouard Manet's *Mademoiselle V ... in the Costume of an Espada* (1862) is one of the most interesting paintings in the collection.
   1. It represents Mademoiselle Victorine dressed as a male bull-fight assistant.
   2. She stares at the viewer, something that pictures like this usually do not do; Manet casts the viewer in the role of the bull.
   3. Manet intended to shock more strongly than Courbet.

V. Camille Pissarro, Claude Monet, Édouard Manet, Pierre-Auguste Renoir, and Edgar Degas created a new, light-filled French painting style that led to Impressionism.

A. Pissarro's *Jalais Hill, Pontoise* (1867) is much like Courbet but more structured in the manner of Corot.

B. Monet's *Garden at Sainte-Adresse* (1867) recalls the Japanese prints that Monet and Degas owned and that the Havemeyers gave to the museum.

C. Manet's *Boating* (1874) is one of the most curious pictures in the museum's collection. The picture is a perplexing work that questions the future.

D. Not all of these young artists were defiant. Renoir's *Madame Georges Charpentier and Her Children* (1878), is a society portrait that shows how ingratiating the Impressionists could be.

E. The Havemeyers' collection of works by Degas is among the greatest in the world.
   1. Degas was the great master of pastels.
   2. *At the Milliner's* (1882) is a modern picture in that everything is cut off at the edges—a new pictorial invention largely motivated by Japanese prints and (as we shall soon see) photography.

VI. Four artists dominated the last two decades of the 19th century, three of whom come directly from Impressionism. These artists were called Postimpressionists and gave form to the appearances they tried to translate into painting.

A. *Circus Sideshow* (1887–1888) by Georges Seurat reminds one of Egyptian art, with its figure's sense of immobility and calmness.

B. Vincent van Gogh fell so in love with the experience of color that his palette changed from one dominated by blacks, browns, and grays to a brilliant, previously unknown pictorial brilliance, as in *Sunflowers* (1887).

C. Paul Cézanne's *The Card Players* (1890–1892) has a monumentality that we have not seen in this entire lecture. Though it has the chromatic brilliance of Delacroix, it has the order of Poussin.

D. Paul Gauguin is the most global artist in the history of art before him.
   1. Made in 1891, the first year of his life in Tahiti, *la Orana Maria (Hail Mary)* represents Mary and Christ as Polynesians.
   2. It is both a Christian and European picture filtered through Gauguin's world travels.

Recommended Reading:

Frelinghuysen. *Splendid Legacy: The Havemeyer Collection.*

Galitzn and Tinterow. *Masterpieces of European Painting in the Metropolitan Museum of Art, 1800–1920.*

Moffett. *Impressionist and Post-Impressionist Paintings in the Metropolitan Museum of Art.*

Questions to Consider:

1. How did Realism rise to dominate French 19th-century painting? Give examples from the museum's collection.

2. The Havemeyers' collection of modern French paintings was one of the museum's most important gifts. What is your favorite work from this collection and why is it important to you?

Lecture Ten
Drawings and Prints

Scope: Of the world's great art museums, only a minority has major holdings of what are called the graphic arts: handmade representations on paper that are either unique or printed. The Metropolitan Museum of Art's collection of graphic arts is among the greatest in the world and includes the entire range of drawing styles and materials from the late Middle Ages to the present as well as superb examples of every Western printing technology from woodcutting through engraving and etching to lithography. With hundreds of thousands of works, these collections are so light sensitive that they are almost always in storage and accessible for study by appointment only. The museum has, however, a large area permanently set aside for changing displays from this rich collection. The selection of works in this lecture will include drawings and prints by the greatest European and American artists of the last six centuries, including Dürer, Rembrandt, Degas, da Vinci, and Ingres.

Outline

I. The Department of Drawings and Prints, created in 1993, has deep roots in the museum.

   A. As the museum's collection of prints, photographs, and drawings of other works of art grew, the museum created the Department of Prints in 1916.

   B. Drawings were kept in the Department of European Paintings and the Department of American Paintings and Sculpture until 1960, when the Department of Drawings was created.

   C. Both departments were assembled into the Department of Drawings and Prints in 1993.

   D. The department has more than 1.5 million objects and is one of the most important holdings of European and American works on paper in the world.

   E. The department is located between two sets of galleries: the Renaissance to 18th-century European paintings and the 19th-century European paintings galleries.

F. William M. Ivins, Jr. was the curator of the department for a long time and was the author of *Prints and Visual Communication*, which focused on the way in which print technology affects the way we see.

    1. Before the 19th century, images were rare, expensive, and difficult to obtain.

    2. The museum's collection reflects the way in which human knowledge has been visualized throughout time.

G. You will have to make an appointment to see many of the works in this collection.

II. Albrecht Dürer was the greatest printmaker during the late 15th and early 16th centuries in all of Europe. No artist had his reach of imagination or produced so many extraordinary prints.

    A. *Samson Rending the Lion* (c. 1497–1498) is a woodcut made from a drawing that a craftsman would cut into wood blocks.

        1. These kinds of prints were printed with type.

        2. If one wanted an amalgam of printing and visual information, the visual information had to be the same height as the type so that it could be set with type and create a connection between word and image.

    B. Dürer was also interested in new kinds of print technology.

        1. *Adam and Eve* (1504) is an engraving of thousands of tiny lines in copper to create an image with a balance of values.

        2. Engravings were harder to print than woodcuts; it was more luxurious and the time it took to create was much longer.

        3. The *Apollo Belvedere* (which had been dug up in Rome a few years before this print was made) is the model for Adam.

III. We skip forward a century and a half later to look at the work of the next great printmaker: Rembrandt van Rijn.

    A. The museum has an almost definitive collection of paintings by Rembrandt and a definitive collection of his prints.

    B. *Christ Crucified between the Two Thieves: The Three Crosses* (1653) was called one of the "100 guilder prints" because it was large enough, difficult enough to print, and rare enough that it cost 100 guilders (almost as much as a painting in the mid-17th century).

        1. The print is about the human response to the Crucifixion.

2. In an etching, a ground is put on the copper plate and etched with a little needle. Then the whole plate is dipped into acid, which etches away the ground where lines are placed.
   3. One can print in a variety of ways (states); in the first state, the two sides of darkness are created by the extraordinary light around Christ.
   4. Every time a plate is redone (reinforced, burnished, altered, re-etched), you have another state.
   5. The fourth state (c. 1660) covers the unrepentant thief in darkness, creating a completely different interpretation of the same scene.

C. Printing is not about the production of identical images from a single plate but about the interpretation of a scene by a great artist and his printers over time.

IV. Now we are going to look at a series of other prints by the great printmakers in the history of art.

A. One of the great printmakers of the 18th century is Giovanni Battista Piranesi, who made prints of Rome's ruins and monuments.
   1. A series of prints made in the mid-18th century, the *Carceri* (prison) series, are prints about imaginary spaces.
   2. *The Round Tower: Plate 3 of Carceri* (c. 1749–1750) looks forward to the prints of 20th-century printmaker M. C. Escher.

B. The most important printmaking technology of the late 18th and 19th centuries was lithography, in which one printed from a lithographic (fine-grained) stone drawn on with grease pencil.
   1. One can print from the stone an infinite number of times because the stone never wears down.
   2. Lithography was developed in Germany in the 18th century and spread rapidly across Europe.
   3. The greatest artist of early lithography was Francisco de Goya y Lucientes, who made a series of prints about bullfighting, *The Bulls of Bordeaux*.
   4. *Picador Caught by a Bull (Bravo toro)* (1825) creates a visual drama that comes from this brand new technology.

C. One of the greatest printmakers of the 19th century was Edgar Degas.
   1. He made many prints called monoprints (one print).

2. *The Fireside* (c. 1876–1877) is a painting made in ink on glass. This image is the first and only impression that would work as a print.

D. Mary Cassatt decided to make a series of prints in color using the European method of etching.

1. The museum has a great set of these etchings because Cassatt was close to Mrs. Havemeyer.

2. One would think that *Woman Bathing* (1890–1891) is a Japanese woodblock print, but the lines are so fine and the color so powdery that the print is much more technically complex.

V. Though the collection of drawings at the museum is smaller, it is equally extraordinary.

A. *Head of the Virgin* (1508–1512) by Leonardo da Vinci is an extraordinarily important drawing representing the head of the Virgin as soft and idealized. This work is a preparatory drawing for a work which hangs in the Louvre.

B. Michelangelo's drawings are as rare as the drawings of da Vinci.

1. *Studies for the Libyan Sibyl (recto)* (1508–1512) depicts the enormous figures meant to hold up the ceiling of the Sistine Chapel.

2. One sees how important this drawing was for the creation of one of the greatest works of Western art.

C. The museum has a series of wonderful drawings made in the 17th century.

1. Giovanni Benedetto Castiglione's *Youth Playing a Pipe for a Satyr* (date unknown) blends drawing and painting; the artist wet a piece of paper with oil and used a brush and pen to make the drawing.

2. Nicolas Poussin's *Bacchanal* (c. 1635–1636), done with brush and ink, relates to the figures in *The Triumph of Pan* (1636) and reflects the ways in which works on paper affect works on canvas.

3. Watteau's *Head of a Man* (c. 1718) illustrates that every great artist has to get from life the character of a figure before actually painting—in this case, before painting *Mezzetin*.

4. Ingres's *The Kaunitz Sisters (Leopoldine, Caroline, and Ferdinandine)* (1818) is a pencil drawing in which he never lifted the pencil as he made the sheet, showing us that when we look at the drawings of great artists, we are in another realm.

5. Turner's *The Lake of Zug* (1843) is one of the 4,000 watercolors he made during his life.

Recommended Reading:

Bean. *100 Drawings in the Metropolitan Museum of Art.*

Ivins. *Prints and Books: Informal Papers.*

Questions to Consider:

1. What is different about the various types of prints (lithograph, etching, woodcut, and engraving)? Which type of print do you prefer and why?

2. What role do drawings have in the creation of other artistic mediums, such as painting or sculpture? Explain this using a drawing discussed in the lecture.

Lecture Eleven
Photographs

Scope: Photography is actually a series of closely related mediums that involve the use of a lens, a small dark space adjacent to it, and a surface—paper, glass, film—that is light sensitive and preserves the scene recorded through the lens. Publicly announced in 1839 in both France and Great Britain, the medium of photography immediately took hold of the European and American imagination and came to dominate image making throughout the world. Although The Metropolitan Museum of Art long collected photography as part of its Department of Drawings and Prints, the sheer scale of the endeavor became so great that, in 1992, the Department of Photography was established with its own headquarters and exhibitions. The collections of this department are of international quality and the lecture will focus on a discreet number of masterpieces by European and American photographers—including Le Gray, Watkins, Eakins, and the protégés of Stieglitz—that chart the evolution of photography from a means of capturing reality to a creative art form in its own right.

Outline

I. Photography is one of the greatest and probably the most pervasive of modern media.

   A. There are many media of photography as there are media of traditional printmaking.

   B. When photography came onto the scene in 1839, it transformed the way human beings related to imagery.

   C. Most great art museums in Europe were impervious to the importance and charms of photography.

II. The Metropolitan Museum of Art was not interested in photography at first.

   A. The museum's print curators collected photographs in the context of collecting prints.

B. Only in 1992 did the museum create the Department of Photography from collections in the Department of Drawings and Prints and, later, through a large amount of purchases.

C. The galleries have changing exhibitions, so you do not see much of the permanent collection (though the changing exhibitions are related to the permanent collection).

D. Only in American art museums are there important collections of photography; openness to new forms of art is something that separates American museums from European ones.

E. I have selected a number of photographs from the beginning of the medium through recent photography. What you should do, however, is see what the museum has at the moment because the quality of its exhibitions is high.

III. The museum has many examples of early photographic work.

    A. The museum has a book created by William Henry Fox Talbot that is probably the most primitive book on photography.

        1. Fox Talbot sensitized sheets of paper with photosensitive compounds to protect them from the light until a certain point to create an image of a botanical specimen from his garden.

        2. *Leaf 8: Peony Leaf* (1839–1840) is a negative image of a leaf and a pure recording of nature.

        3. Fox Talbot waxed the negative image, put it on another sheet of sensitized paper, and made a positive image called a calotype.

        4. The museum has very important holdings of this early negative/positive photographic process.

    B. The daguerreotype, the opposite of Fox Talbot's invention, was introduced in Paris in 1839.

        1. The daguerreotype is a unique print on silvered photosensitized metal; it is a positive image that cannot be reproduced.

        2. Daguerreotypes were oftentimes used for portraits, as in the American daguerreotype *Lemuel Shaw* (c. 1850) by Albert Sands Southworth and Josiah Johnson Hawes.

        3. These shiny prints are so exact that one can see all the subject's flaws.

IV. These two photographic techniques worked equally well all over the world.

A. Americans used daguerreotypes for portraits, while the British and French were interested in paper photography.

B. Gustave Le Gray was a painter who began to make photographs as part of the painting process and eventually became a professional photographer.

    1. *Oak Tree and Rocks, Forest of Fontainebleau* (1849–1852) is a blurry calotype project more like art.

    2. About 20 years earlier, Corot was doing the same thing with paint on paper in *Fontainebleau: Oak Trees at Bas-Bréau* (1832 or 1833) so that, from the beginning, photography was intertwined with art and painting.

C. The United States was fascinated with the western landscape of which those in the east were unaware; both photographers and painters went west to depict what the country looked like.

    1. Carleton Watkins worked in the new medium of wet-plate collodium with a negative made of glass.

    2. *View on the Columbia, Cascades* (1867) is one of thousands of glass plates that Watkins made in his life.

D. In France, the photographer Félix Nadar (whose actual name was Gaspard-Félix Tournachon) photographed the rich and famous of the Second Empire. *Pierrot Laughing* (1885) is a photograph of a mime who had to stand still long enough for Nadar to take his picture.

V. The idea of realistic, dispassionate portrait photography is important in the history of art during the mid-19th century.

A. Louis-Rémy Robert's *Alfred Thompson Gobert* (1849–1855) displays a complete control of the relationship between light and dark and a respectful sense of the sitter.

B. The museum has extraordinary mid-19th-century portraits from Germany, France, England, and the United States.

C. Julia Margaret Cameron was the first great female photographer.

    1. Her photograph of the novelist Virginia Woolf's mother, *Julia Jackson* (1867), depicts a haunted, naïve beauty in a young woman who just stares at the viewer.

    2. Head-on shots like this are quite large and approach the scale of actual figures.

VI. In the United States, photography was used quite a lot by artists.

A. Thomas Eakins used photography the most creatively.

    1. *Thomas Eakins and John Laurie Wallace at the Shore* (c. 1883) is a posed shot used for Eakins's studies of the nude human body.

    2. There are many photographs in Eakins's career that are incredibly poetic and constructed as lost narratives.

B. American photography received an enormous boost from Alfred Stieglitz, the first great entrepreneur of artistic photography.

    1. One of his most important students and protégés was Edward Steichen, whose *The Flatiron* (1904; printed 1909) is about atmosphere and art. It was one of the great prints in one of the first and most important exhibits of photography in America: the International Exhibition of Pictorial Photography.

    2. Stieglitz's *Georgia O'Keeffe* (1918) creates an erotic, sensual modesty from the diagonal lines that converge at the subject's lips.

    3. Paul Strand, another friend and protégé, made three great donations to the museum, including *Blind* (1916). He realized that if he pointed the camera at someone, he or she would not want to be photographed; thus, he made a camera that took a picture from the side.

C. Lewis W. Hine was a New York photographer interested in social justice.

    1. He photographed immigrants in squalid conditions, underage workers, and men in factories.

    2. *Steamfitter* (1921) is a slightly romanticized image in which he obviously looks toward the creation of visual beauty.

D. Eugène Atget took thousands of photographs of areas in Paris that he knew would not last; an example of this is *Shop front of "Courone d'or," Quai Bourbon* (1922).

E. Walker Evans was interested in photographing an immediate composition and responding to the photographic surface in works like *Floyd and Lucille Burroughs on Porch, Hale County, Alabama* (1936).

F. Man Ray's photographs, like *Compass* (1920), are visual jokes. He made what he called "rayograms," in which he put various objects on sensitized paper and made combinative images.

G. Garry Winogrand used a Lica camera with a fast exposure time to make thousands of photographs a day, hoping for one good shot such as *El Morocco* (1955).

Recommended Reading:

Hambourg. "Photography between Wars: Selections from the Ford Motor Company Collection."

Naef. *The Collection of Alfred Stieglitz: Fifty Pioneers of Modern Photography.*

Questions to Consider:

1. Why was Alfred Stieglitz important to the history of the museum?
2. Choose a photograph from the collection and describe why it is important both to you and to the museum's collection.

Lecture Twelve
European Decorative Arts

Scope: In spite of the fact that a majority of Americans are of European origin, travel to Europe was, until recently, a luxury reserved either for college students or the rich. For that reason, it was thought important by the directors and trustees of The Metropolitan Museum of Art to provide the public with a chance to understand the full range of European luxury goods and the environments for which they were created to complement the fine arts (painting and sculpture). The collections of decorative arts—including ceramics, glass, metalwork, jewelry, and wooden objects (what the museum has traditionally called "minor arts")—are housed in galleries adjacent to a large collection of rooms made from paneling, windows, doors, and architectural elements from original European settings. These vary from an Italian Renaissance *studiolo* with superb paneling and a grand formal dining room from 18th-century England to a Neoclassical drawing room from the south of France. These rooms are generally furnished with appropriate period objects—though not necessarily from the same house or building. The resulting environments allow the visitor to travel through time and space without leaving New York City. The lecture will introduce a small sample of the most provocative period environments as well as a group of individual masterpieces of decorative art.

Outline

I. To the left of the main staircase is a double-storied hall that leads to the Department of European Decorative Arts and Sculpture, arranged in a huge suite of galleries and comprising the museum's largest real estate after the Department of European Paintings.

    A. If you do not mind getting delightfully lost, it is best to follow your instincts and wander through the groups of rooms.

        1. You will go through a kind of time travel that is one of the most pleasurable aspects of going to the museum.

        2. The galleries are full of atmosphere because most of them are period rooms.

B. J. P. Morgan was a trustee of the museum between 1904 and 1913 and was responsible for the museum's acquisition of period rooms. The period rooms are based on his supposition that most Americans came from Europe and thus there should be places of the imagination for Americans who cannot afford to go back.

C. Period rooms are difficult to discuss because none of them are exactly accurate.

    1. It is best to forget about accuracy because that is not why the rooms are there.

    2. The rooms are there for you to dream, imagine encounters, and think about the ways that earlier people lived.

II. I am going to take you into some of the period rooms, but to get the best impression of the collection you need to visit the museum.

    A. One of the most wonderful period rooms in the museum is also one of the smallest and most ambitious: Studiolo from the Ducal Palace in Gubbio, Italy (c. 1478–1482).

        1. Francesco di Giorgio Martini designed the *studiolo* as an irregular anteroom.

        2. The room is just flat pieces of wood placed together to form a pictorial mosaic of things; the entire *studiolo* is an illusion executed by Giuliano da Maiano.

        3. The room is a portrait of its owner's ambitions, knowledge, and world.

        4. One can find places in the room where everything converges on a point.

    B. The bedroom from the Sagredo Palace in Venice (c. 1718) is a room of unbelievable elaborateness and expense. As reflected in the ceiling painting representing Aurora, goddess of the dawn, the room is about waking up rather than going to sleep.

    C. One of the most popular rooms throughout the museum's history is the so-called "Swiss Room," bought by the Rogers Fund shortly after J. P. Morgan became a trustee of the museum.

        1. The 17th-century room's stove (c. 1684–1685) is attributed to David II Pfau.

        2. The room is so richly carved that one can look at all the woodcarvings and decipher what the room meant to the owner.

III. In addition, The Metropolitan Museum of Art has period rooms from England.

   A. The period room from a house on the Hall Quay in Great Yarmouth, Norfolk, England, is the room of a merchant named Crowe.

   1. The room's paneling and chimneypiece (c. 1600) illustrate the room's wonderful carving.

   2. By looking at one of the museum's American rooms (built 30 or 40 years later than this), one can see the distance between provincial England and provincial America in the 17th century.

   B. Eighteenth-century England's fascination with the Grand Tour and sophistication is reflected in the grand formal dining room from Kirtlington Park (1748).

   1. The museum built the room from various pieces brought to New York City in the early 1930s.

   2. The room is furnished as a reception room, which it was not intended to be, so one has to think differently about it when one visits.

   C. A period room belonging to an infinitely richer man, the Sixth Earl of Coventry, is the Tapestry Room from Croome Court (c. 1760–1769).

   1. Robert Adam designed the ceiling with its Neoclassical decoration, which is not so thick as the decoration in the Kirtlington Park dining room.

   2. One sees that the circle in the rug is the same proportion as the circle in the ceiling, making the room fit together as a unit.

   3. Adam also designed the Lansdowne House dining room (1765–1768), a pretentious and insufferably grand room.

IV. The French rooms at the museum are so detailed that I have restricted myself to discussing one.

   A. *Boiserie* from the Hôtel de Cabris (c. 1775–1778 and later) was made in Paris but located in southern French town named Grasse.

   B. Each object in this room is of perfect taste. We have gotten away from grandeur and pretension and are in a realm of heightened refinement that existed a scant 20 years before the French Revolution.

V. The museum also has galleries reserved exclusively for masterpieces of decorative art.

A. Since the mid-19th century, American museums have thought that great pieces of furniture, metalwork, fireplace screens, silver, settees, and other pieces are worth as much to our appreciation of past cultures as paintings and sculpture.

    1. Museums of decorative or applied arts in European cities are in different places from fine arts museums.

    2. In the museum's period rooms, there is an integration of all the arts for form and environment and a sense that some works of decorative arts are of such high quality that they need to be looked at as if they were paintings or sculptures.

B. A commode (c. 1710–1732) by André-Charles Boulle reflects a style of furniture developed for the reign of King Louis XIV.

    1. Louis XIV commissioned French artists to surpass the work they had studied abroad to create a new French style that was at a higher level than anyone else.

    2. Boulle would make matching pieces of furniture in which the background was sometimes pewter, tortoiseshell, or brass; then he would create variations of the combined materials.

    3. This style of commode was so popular that other aristocrats commissioned them from Boulle.

C. A 1783 desk by Jean-Henri Riesener was made for Marie Antoinette, the last Bourbon queen of France. It is a writing desk that possesses a sense of suffocating luxury, beauty, and perfection.

D. The armoire by Charles-Guillaume Diehl and Jean Brandely (1867) is an extraordinary piece of furniture with a scene of the first victory of civilization over barbarism after the fall of the Roman Empire: the defeat of Attila the Hun by King Merovech in 451.

    1. The beginning of civilization after Rome is shown in silver; the rest of the work is in wood.

    2. The work possesses such unbelievable vulgarity and quality that it makes one realize that French craftsmanship never faltered after the death of Boulle in 1832.

Recommended Reading:

Koda. *Dangerous Liaisons: Fashion and Furniture in the Eighteenth Century.*

Peck. *Period Rooms in the Metropolitan Museum of Art.*

Questions to Consider:

1. Of the period rooms presented in this lecture, which is your favorite and why?

2. How does taking a decorative art piece (such as a ceramic, a piece of jewelry, or a piece of furniture) out of its original context affect its meaning and appearance?

Lecture Thirteen
European Sculpture

Scope: The collection of European sculpture from the Middle Ages through the 19th century is housed mostly among the period rooms and decorative arts galleries on the ground floor of The Metropolitan Museum of Art. Although not nearly as comprehensive as the museum's collection of paintings from the same period, it is of national significance and includes major medieval altarpieces, superb Renaissance sculpture in stone, bronze, and terracotta, and masterpieces of Baroque sculpture by artists such as Bernini, Foggini, Canova, and others. The collection strengthens considerably in the 18th and 19th centuries, and there is scarcely a major European sculptor during this time period who is unrepresented by a masterpiece. The lecture will consider the rise of sculpture in the 15th century as an independent medium in competition with painting and will consider the evolution of the sculptor's various materials through the work of Rodin and Degas.

Outline

I. The most important of the three-dimensional arts is sculpture.

    A. In many museums, sculpture is segregated from the decorative arts.

        1. At The Metropolitan Museum of Art, two-dimensional objects are on the second floor, and three-dimensional objects are on the first floor.

        2. The history of art suggests a battle between making something in three dimensions or creating an illusion on a two-dimensional surface.

    B. The sculptures at the museum are contained in a naturally lit space because sculpture looks best out of doors.

II. The Metropolitan Museum of Art has major masterpieces throughout the course of European sculpture.

    A. *Madonna and Child with Angels* (15th century) by Antonio Rossellino is a low-relief sculpture.

        1. The combination of real shadows and illusionary lines gives a sense that one is looking at both a sculpture and a painting.

2. Unlike many marble sculptures from the Renaissance and early Baroque period, this sculpture maintains its original surface and original gilding.

B. *Virgin and Child* (15th century) by Andrea della Robbia reflects the artist's mode of working with glazed ceramic sculpture.
   1. He would put pure colored glazes on various parts of a ceramic sculpture in a manner similar to the two panels of striding lions in the Department of Ancient Near Eastern Art.
   2. This work is a high relief sculpture that creates the corporeality of the Virgin and Christ Child.
   3. The sculpture creates a psychological bond between mother and child that makes the work tenderer than Rossellino's.

III. The collections at The Metropolitan Museum of Art have a huge shift in time from the 15th century to the beginning of the 17th century.

A. The greatest sculptor of the 17th century was Gian Lorenzo Bernini.
   1. The only great full-scale marble sculpture by Bernini in America is at The Metropolitan Museum of Art.
   2. *Bacchanal: A Faun Teased by Children* (c. 1616–1617) is a carved bacchanal like the drawn bacchanals of Poussin and Castiglione.
   3. Unlike Egyptian, Greek, and Roman sculpture, this work is about motion; from every single viewpoint, the work is a different sculpture.
   4. There is a sense in which there is change and transformation in the sculpted image in the 17th century, just as there is in the painted image.

B. Giovanni Battista Foggini was a Florentine artist who worked with Bernini.
   1. As the official sculptor of the Medici family, he created *Grand Prince Ferdinando de' Medici (1663–1713)* around 1683 to 1685.
   2. We think of busts as relatively inert, but here the drapery, hair, and lace collar seem in the midst of a rustling wind.

C. Jean-Louis Lemoyne was the most important French sculptor of the first half of the 17th century.
   1. *La Crainte des Traits de l'Amour* (1739–1740) is a life-size female figure clad in a Roman way so that we see her as a goddess.

       2.   Unlike the Bernini sculpture, this work was meant to be seen only from the front; it has more of the qualities of a picture frozen in marble than a real sculpture that you move around.

IV. Portrait busts are the representations of people in sculpted form.

    A. Jean-Antoine Houdon was the greatest French sculptor of the late 18th and early 19th centuries.

        1. *Sabine Houdon* (1788) is a tiny portrait bust of the artist's daughter that measures 10½ inches high.

        2. The work is one of the earliest sculptural portraits of a child.

    B. *Madame de Wailly* (1789) was sculpted by Augustin Pajou, Houdon's rival at the end of the 18th century.

        1. The Roman style of dress is both Classical and erotic.

        2. This bust is the result of centuries of rethinking and reworking the traditions of European marble sculpture.

    C. Antonio Canova's *Perseus with the Head of Medusa* (1804–1806) is a life-size male nude sculpted in perfect white marble.

        1. With this figure, modern sculpture finally reaches a higher plateau of style and perfection than ancient sculpture.

        2. Canova hollowed the head of Medusa and contrived the elegant drapery to carry the weight of the outstretched arm, reflecting the attention paid to engineering.

        3. Looking at the heads of Medusa and Perseus, one sees a careful observation in the midst of all this idealization.

        4. The work was commissioned by the Pope to be seen with the Apollo Belvedere (c. 350–320 B.C.), the most perfect sculpture of antiquity.

    D. Jean-Baptiste Carpeaux's *Ugolino and His Sons* (modeled 1860–1861; executed 1865–1867) is a sculpture taken from Dante's *Inferno*.

        1. Like Bernini's sculpture, this is a 360-degree sculpture; as one walks around it, one sees the relationship between each figure.

        2. Ugolino's pose was the source for Rodin's *The Thinker* (1880).

    E. Edgar Degas made more than 100 sculptures in wax during his lifetime, only one of which he exhibited: *The Little Fourteen-Year-Old Dancer* (executed c. 1880; cast in 1922).

        1. The museum's piece is cast in bronze; the original was in mixed media.

2. Everything we know about Degas's sculpture comes from Mrs. Havemeyer, who gave a complete set of bronzes to the museum.

F. Auguste Rodin's terracotta portrait *Honoré de Balzac* (probably 1891) helps us think about the way in which the embodiment of a particular individual in sculptural form can be more powerful than any painting.
   1. Rodin made studies of Balzac's death mask, of which this bust is one.
   2. The work makes one think about the head of a ruler in the museum's Department of Near Eastern Art.

Recommended Reading:

Pope-Hennesy. *The Study and Criticism of Italian Sculpture.*

Tinterow. *The New Nineteenth-Century European Paintings and Sculpture Galleries.*

Questions to Consider:

1. What medium of sculpture is your favorite? Explain why it is your favorite using one of the sculptures studied in this lecture.
2. Who is your favorite sculptor represented in the museum and why?

Lecture Fourteen
The Arts of Africa and Oceania

Scope: The Metropolitan Museum of Art was, like many other great art museums, rather late in accepting the arts of Africa, Oceania, and the Americas into its representation of world art. It was only with the merging of the independent Museum of Primitive Art with The Metropolitan Museum of Art that a major department was formed which combined The Metropolitan Museum of Art's scattered holdings with the major collections established at the Museum of Primitive Art by the Rockefeller family. When the Department of the Arts of Africa, Oceania and the Americas opened its galleries in the Michael C. Rockefeller Wing in 1982, years of aesthetic prejudice were wiped away, and New Yorkers could consider the diverse tribal and highly urban art forms of these three continents as a major contribution to world civilization. There is no doubt, however, that the collections of this single department are more diverse than those of any other in the museum, making it all the more difficult to boil them down to a manageable number that is a fair sample of the whole. For that reason, this lecture is devoted to the fundamentally tribal cultures of Africa and Oceania, with some attention paid to the highly developed urban cultures of north-central Africa (particular that of Benin); the next lecture will be devoted to art from the ancient New World. It is no accident that the galleries for these cultures are located adjacent to those for 20th-century art—in the late 19th and early 20th centuries modern Western artists were inspired by the arts of Africa and Oceania.

Outline

I. The cultures of Oceania, Africa, and the ancient New World are brilliantly represented at The Metropolitan Museum of Art.

   A. These cultures came to the museum rather late in its history.

   B. In traditional fine arts museums, the idea was that these cultures did not produce art at all but instead artifacts that belonged in natural history museums.

C. In the 20th century, artists began to discover the great riches of these cultures; these discoveries began to be communicated through modern art to many people around the world.

D. The arts of Oceania and Africa came to the museum in 1969 through the Rockefeller family.
1. The Rockefellers started their own private museum called the Museum of Primitive Art.
2. In memory of Michael Rockefeller, the family gave their collection to The Metropolitan Museum of Art; in 1982, the Michael C. Rockefeller Wing opened.

E. The collection's galleries are dimly lit because its holdings (made of various woods, pigments, and feathers) would fade in bright sunlight.

II. The region of Oceania spans Papua New Guinea to Australia and includes the tip of New Zealand and island groups including the Easter Islands and the Galapagos Islands.

A. The Maori feather box (c. 18th century) is a very rare carved-wood object that reflects the magical powers many of the collection's objects were made for.

B. The mask (19th century) is a turtleshell mask from the Torres Straits.
1. Many of these objects were destroyed when Westerners came to the islands; this is one of only two surviving masks of this type.
2. When you look at an object with unknown origins like this, it allows you to interpret the work in extraordinary ways.

C. I want to contrast an object from the western Pacific Islands and an object from the eastern Pacific Islands.
1. The standing male figure (Tiki) (18th–early 19th century) is a rare object from the Gambier Islands, correctly carved in terms of anatomical detail.
2. The Moai Tangata (early 19th century) was made on Easter Island; its realism, perfect proportions, mysterious meaning, and physical power are extraordinary.

D. The Solomon Islands produced wonderful objects like a ceremonial shield from the early to mid-19th century covered with thin pigments and inlaid with fragments of shell.

E. The helmet mask (mid–20th century), represents one of the early mythical female cannibals of the Mbotgote island group; the great form that the woman gives birth to is the mask itself.

F. The museum contains works from the island of New Guinea.
   1. The skull hook, or Agiba (19th–early 20th century), was used to hold the skulls of enemies from another village.
   2. Bis poles (mid-20th century) were a type of memorial pole carved like a boat; boats frequently appear in work from these water-based cultures.

G. Almost all of these objects were made to be used.

III. The urgency of form (e.g., exaggerated facial features, exaggerated proportions) expressed in the work of non-Western cultures gave early-20th-century artists the idea that they did not have to follow the Greco-Roman forms of the Western tradition.

IV. The museum's collection of African art has a greater depth of time.

A. The seated figure (13th century) has a formal originality that makes us look at it in a new way.

B. The 16th-century pendant mask, made by the Edo people, was given to the museum by Nelson Rockefeller in 1972.
   1. The museum has many Benin bronzes.
   2. The mask's headdress is a series of Portuguese soldiers (who traded with the Benin people).

C. The seated couple (16th–19th century) was made by the Dogan people. One can imagine a whole series of works of modern art that stem from this couple.

D. The 19th-century prestige stool was made by an artist called the Buli Master, possibly an artist named Ngongo ya Chintu.

E. African art scholarship in Europe, America, and increasingly in Africa is able to identify particular artists whose work can be studied in relationship to artists before them.
   1. The department has a library formed by Robert Goldwater.
   2. Knowledge has incrementally increased during the time these objects have been in the museum because the works are able to be seen by scholars.

F. The male power figure (19th–20th century) wears the particular sufferings and problems of its owner. There are many objects of this type in America, many of them forgeries.

G. The museum has two masks that are important for modern art.
   1. The mask made by the Senufo people between the 19th and 20th centuries is the kind of head found in works by Modernists like Modigliani.
   2. The reliquary head, made between the 19th and 20th centuries by the Fang people in Gabon, reminds one of Brancusi's work; its purity and form made Modernists want to change art forever.

Recommended Reading:

Douglas. *Art of Africa, the Pacific Islands, and the Americas.*

Kjellgren. *Oceania: Art of the Pacific Islands in The Metropolitan Museum of Art.*

LaGamma. *Art and Oracle: African Art and Rituals of Divination.*

Questions to Consider:

1. How was the Rockefeller family influential in the development of the museum's galleries of African and Oceanic art?
2. How were early 19th- and 20th- century artists influenced by the arts of Africa and Oceania? What work in the museum's collection illustrates this connection?

Lecture Fifteen
The Ancient New World

Scope: The Rockefeller donation, rich in the arts of Africa and Oceania, lured other collectors who specialized in art from the ancient New World. By 1982, The Metropolitan Museum of Art had important works from all the major civilizations of the pre-European New World. From the cultures of what is now Peru through the village-based, metallurgy-producing cultures of northern South and Central America to the successive urban civilizations of ancient Mexico, Guatemala, and the southwestern United States, these collections comprise the most comprehensive display of ancient New World art in a general art museum anywhere in the world. This lecture will explore the work of ancient Mexico's Olmec, Maya, and Aztec cultures, works from cultures with markedly less urban grandeur such as Costa Rica and Peru, and rarities from the museum's collection of work from Caribbean and Eskimo cultures.

Outline

I. Most art museums have very few works of pre-Hispanic (formerly pre-Colombian) art. The museum is fortunate enough to possess a collection of works that lay bare the depth of civilization in the Americas.

   A. The Department of Africa, Oceania, and the Americas has a series of galleries devoted to the Americas.

   B. These galleries have mostly portage objects; there are very few monumental objects that give one a sense of the grandeur of these civilizations.

II. We are going to look at a few masterpieces by the major cultures of the ancient New World, starting with Mexico.

   A. In the 1920s, there was a reform in Mexican education under Minister of Education José Vasconcelos that stressed a respect of Mexican history by making a connection to the ancient Mediterranean.
      1. The equivalents to the Egyptians were the Olmecs.
      2. The equivalents to the Greeks were the Maya.
      3. The equivalents to the Romans were the Aztecs.

4. The museum has examples of Olmec, Mayan, and Aztec art.

B. The Olmec "baby" figure (12th–9th century B.C.) is made of white slip ceramic and is one of the most complex ceramic objects we have seen.

    1. The figure's mouth is oftentimes interpreted by scholars as the mouth of a jaguar.

    2. This work is part of a population of white hollowware ceramic babies.

C. The jade carvings of the Olmecs, including an Olmec mask (10th–6th century B.C.), are of extraordinary quality; however, we know little about where they come from and, hence, what they mean.

D. Both Olmec objects show that the people of the ancient New World were as technologically proficient as any ancient people.

E. The "smiling" figure (7th–8th century) is a hollowware ceramic object made by the Remojadas people.

    1. All their ceramics are made with a slip over the costume elements and a red pigment over the skin.

    2. Objects like this were tomb burial objects.

    3. This is one of the first objects we have seen that represents humor or mirth convincingly; you have to go to Frans Hals's *Young Man and Woman in an Inn ("Yonker Ramp and His Sweetheart")* to find a similar expression in Western art.

F. The Maya, like the Greeks, had no centralized authority but were composed of various city-states with its own scribes, artists, and architects.

    1. Only a few wooden sculptures, such as the Mirror-Bearer (6th century), survive. The Maya had the ability to convey emotion through physiognomy, an important ability in the history of art.

    2. The Maya were the first and only people in the ancient New World to develop a system of writing; deciphering this writing has made it possible for scholars to understand what objects mean.

    3. The Maya were great painters of vessels, including a vessel depicting a mythological scene (8th century).

    4. Many pots were signed by the painters who made them, suggesting that painters were appreciated as artists.

G. The Aztec people came from the north of Mexico into the central valley, creating their capital of Tenochtitlan (modern-day Mexico

City); because the city was destroyed by the Spanish, few elements survive.

1. One of them is a seated standard bearer (second half of the 15th century–early 16th century) which recalls the sandstone sculpture produced in ancient Egypt.

2. Almost all of Aztec sculpture is rare outside of Mexico; seeing a sculpture of this level and scale at The Metropolitan Museum of Art is almost impossible anywhere else in the United States.

III. We are going to look at a number of objects that do not come from civilizations with the same urban grandeur as the ones we have previously looked at.

A. The frog pendant (11th–16th century) was produced in Costa Rica and is part of a population of pendants depicting a certain type of tree frog used as a hallucinogen for vision quests.

B. A lime container (*poporo*) from 1st–7th-century Colombia held crushed seashells used to produce hallucinogenic reactions in shamans.

C. The seated figure (1st century B.C.–A.D. 1st century) is a figure from Colombia or Ecuador that represents a sense of motion and urgency.

D. The Peruvian collections at the museum divide themselves between ceramics and metals.

1. The single-spouted feline-head bottle (9th–5th century B.C.) from the Tembladera culture has an incredibly sophisticated originality of production unlike anything we have seen in China or other parts of the world.

2. The feline incense vessel (6th–9th century) from the Tiwanaku culture may be a family symbol.

3. The Nazca culture produced multi-spouted pots like the double-spout bottle (2nd–4th century).

4. Gold metallurgy in Peru was extraordinary, and the museum's collections include a Sicán funerary mask (10th–11th century).

5. The collection also has extraordinary silver objects, including a deer vessel (14th–15th century) from the Chimú region; silver was associated with pre-Hispanic Peruvians.

IV. A small part of the collection deals with works of art from the Caribbean Islands, the Eskimo regions of the Arctic, and Native American civilizations; the museum has a few rarities.

    A. The 15th–16th-century deity figure (*Zemi*) is made of ironwood inlaid with shell. It was produced by the Taino people, who lived on the islands around the Dominican Republic.

    B. It is no accident that the Surrealists loved Eskimo masks like the early-20th-century dance mask; American sculptor Alexander Calder took his impetus from Eskimo objects.

Recommended Reading:

Douglas. *Art of Africa, the Pacific Islands, and the Americas.*

O'Neill. *Mexico: Splendors of Thirty Centuries.*

Questions to Consider:

1. Based upon the objects studied in this session, what pre-Hispanic culture of the Americas attracts you most and why?

2. What object in this lecture has given you a new appreciation for the people of the ancient New World and why?

Lecture Sixteen
Musical Instruments and Arms and Armor

Scope: Few great European national museums have collections either of
musical instruments or of arms and armor—the former tend to be
in palace museums or separate museums of the decorative arts, the
latter in royal or military museums. In a nation without a medieval
or Renaissance military, however, there are few better places to
place armor than The Metropolitan Museum of Art. Hence, the
museum's great collections of both these areas of "the useful arts"
(the arts of war and the arts of the hunt and of peace) are housed in
a suite of galleries directly adjacent to the Department of European
Sculpture and Decorative Arts' galleries. The collections are
highly specialized and important in their own right and deserve the
separation maintained by The Metropolitan Museum of Art. The
lecture will deal with major masterpieces in the Department of
Arms and Armor and the Department of Musical Instruments,
treating swords, pistols, pianos, and guitars as important works of
art worthy of study and admiration.

Outline

I. Two of the most fun, glorious, and educational parts of The
Metropolitan Museum of Art to visit are the Department of Arms and
Armor (on the museum's ground floor) and the Department of Musical
Instruments (on the museum's second floor).

II. The Department of Arms and Armor contains a specialized collection
of global arms and armor, with an emphasis on Europe and Japan.

    A. The galleries make you want to go into the rest of the museum and
think about the arts of war as represented in other collections.

    B. The Metropolitan Museum of Art has one of the great curatorial
departments of arms and armor, though the Philadelphia Museum,
the Art Institute of Chicago, and the Cleveland Museum have
collections.

    C. The sallet (1470–1480) is an extraordinary helmet made of steel
and covered with copper gilt.

        1. People in Renaissance Italy wanted to look like the ancients,
just as they wanted to paint and sculpt like the ancients.

2. The helmet's representation of the mythological Nemean Lion makes it a symbol of the wearer's power.

D. Burgonet with Falling Buffe (c. 1555) was made in the great armory of the Louvre.
  1. All the major imperial European powers had their own armorers who competed with each other to make their rulers look the best.
  2. Armorers of the late 14th and early 15th century employed the same techniques used to engrave and etch metal prints.
  3. Helmets like these would have very little effect from a distance; up close, it is just as complex as any engraving.
  4. This helmet was given by the king of France to Cosimo II; the museum has in its permanent collection a portrait of Cosimo II in which this helmet sits as an imperial gift.

E. The museum has wonderful examples of full suits of European armor. In certain parts of the museum you will see a whole set of armor and, around it, the various parts that compose that set.
  1. The armor of George Clifford, Third Earl of Cumberland (c. 1580–1585), shows how pervasive was the advanced technology of armor-making and weapon-making in Europe during this time.
  2. There was a whole group of artists who only decorated the armor.
  3. There are a lot of paintings in the European galleries of 14th- and 15th-century painting that show men in armor (such as Cranach the Elder's *The Judgment of Paris*, possibly from around 1528).
  4. It is interesting to compare the collection of armor in the museum with the armor in the galleries of painting.

F. The Department of Arms and Armor has one of the best collections of Japanese armor in the United States.
  1. One sample of armor (*gusoku*) from the 16th and 18th centuries shows how different Japanese armor is from European armor: it is lighter, designed to encourage the movement of the knight underneath, and designed to shock and awe the enemy.
  2. Japanese armor could be adapted as technology changed.
  3. One can learn an enormous amount about the Japanese mind and military technology by looking at a Japanese suit of armor and comparing it to a suit of European armor.

    G. The museum has a fantastic collection of swords.
- **1.** Presentation Smallsword (1798–1799) by James Morisset was meant to be an object not of violence but of power.
- **2.** The 19th-century saber was made in the Ottoman Empire to be the equivalent honor of a royal crown in Europe. The blade came from an Iranian sword and the jade handle was Indian, suggesting the depth of time and reach of the Ottoman Empire.

    H. The museum also has a unique collection of pistols.
- **1.** Double-Barreled Wheellock Pistol of Emperor Charles V (c. 1540–1545) by Ambrosius Gemlich and Peter Pech is so detailed that one could view it with a magnifying glass.
- **2.** The Samuel Colt revolver (c. 1853) has very American designs (including George Washington and American mammals) crafted by Gustave Young.

    I. There are wonderful shields as well, including a tournament shield (*targe*) from around 1450 and a symbolic shield (c. 1535) painted on wood and never meant to be used.

III. The gallery of musical instruments, located upstairs, is equally fun.

    A. The double virginal (1581) is one of the earliest keyboard instruments that survives. Though made in Antwerp for the king of Spain, it was found in a country house in Peru and acquired by the museum in 1929.

    B. Michele Todini's harpsichord (c. 1675) is a modern instrument that uses ancient and mythological prototypes. One can imagine this harpsichord in the museum's Venetian period bedroom.

    C. One of the museum's most important instruments does not look like a great work of art: Bartolomeo Christofori's grand piano (1720). The piece is the earliest surviving pianoforte and displays an extraordinary use of the technology of sound rather than physical beauty.

    D. The museum has other kinds of string instruments as well.
- **1.** Matteo Sellas's guitar (c. 1630–1650) is strung as it would have been at the time of its creation.
- **2.** One of the rarest instruments in the world is a 1693 violin by Antonio Stradivari, which is still in the condition it was when it was made.

    E. The museum's musical instruments are not all European.

1. The 19th-century *mayuri* is an Indian instrument probably made for a Hindu court; it is from the Crosby Brown collection—the great collection of musical instruments that came to the museum in 1889.
2. *Rag-Dung* was a Ming Dynasty (1368–1644) instrument used in Tibet for important rituals at Buddhist temples.
3. This *sho*, a 19th-century Japanese flute played laterally, depicts a charming lacquered scene of a spider and a cricket below its bamboo pipes.
4. Charles Joseph Sax's Clarinet in B-flat (1830) is made of elephant ivory.
5. *Bondjo* (c. 1915) is an African transverse flute meant to embody sound; the shapes are also the same as those on the crown of this particular tribe's king.
6. *O-daiko* (c. 1873) is a Japanese drum made to be sent to the 1873 World's Fair in Austria, where Japan displayed its prowess to the great European nations.

Recommended Reading:

Dean. *Helmets And Body Armor In Modern Warfare: The Metropolitan Museum Of Art.*

Libin. *Our Tuneful Heritage: American Musical Instruments from The Metropolitan Museum of Art.*

Nickel, Pyhrr, and Tarassuk. *Art of Chivalry: European Arms and Armor from the Metropolitan Museum of Art: An Exhibition.*

Questions to Consider:

1. Should art museums have a department for musical instruments? Why or why not?
2. Is there a need for all encyclopedic art museums to have a gallery of arms and armor? Why or why not?

Lecture Seventeen
Costumes and Textiles

Scope: Although every great universal art museum collects textiles, few
museums extend their collections to fashion or costume art.
Because of New York City's international prominence as a center
for fashion design and retail, however, The Metropolitan Museum
of Art created a separate department called the Costume Institute in
1937, which united the museum's various holdings in Western
costumes from the late 16th through the early 21st centuries. The
institute is treated as a resource for professionals, retailers,
costume designers, and other experts who consult its files, library,
photo-archive, and storage collections. In the 1980s, the Costume
Institute inaugurated a permanent space for its exhibitions, some
based on their collections and others curated by the staff to expand
knowledge of costume art to the larger public. What once had been
a scholarly department for specialists has become one of the most
visible centers for the exhibition of fashionable clothing in the
world. The Costume Institute, however, contains a minority of the
vast collections of textiles controlled by other departments at The
Metropolitan Museum of Art. These textiles—from immense
Flemish tapestries and Islamic carpets to small samples of
Venetian velvets and French silks—are catalogued and conserved
in the Antonio Ratti Textile Center.

Outline

I. This lecture is devoted to two departments at the museum, one of which
has gallery spaces and the other of which only has a study center: the
Costume Institute and the Antonio Ratti Textile Center, respectively.

   A. These are among the most important collections of textiles and
costumes in any museum in the world.

   B. In 1937, the Lewisohn family started its own independent costume
institute in New York City. The collection became so widely used
and so important that the institute came to The Metropolitan
Museum of Art in 1959.

   C. The textile collection includes more than 30,000 objects such as
shoes, belts, buckles, dresses, trousers, and hats. It is to be used by

people who need to be inspired by the past: clothing designers, retailers, set designers, and costume designers.

D. The Costume Institute's galleries are located on the museum's ground floor. You will not see the galleries' permanent collection but instead an exhibition derived from the collection along with loaned objects.

II. We will review a sample of objects from the Costume Institute, mostly European and American, to illustrate the range and quality of The Metropolitan Museum of Art's holdings.

    A. A doublet from the early 1620s was made in France and painstakingly embroidered so that it has, for us today, a decidedly feminine quality.

        1. What makes it possible to date this object are the slits of contrasting silk in the sleeves and bodice, called pinking; male garments were pinked for only a five-year period in the early 1620s.

        2. There are only two garments of this type in the world that survived: this one, and one in the Victoria and Albert Museum in London.

    B. Early shoes are rare; one sees them more in paintings than in real form.

        1. The collection includes a pair of 17th-century men's shoes made for silk-stockinged legs.

        2. The cantilever suggests that men kept the weight of their body on their toes.

    C. The court dress (c. 1750) is the type of dress worn in European courts in the mid-18th century. The dress, with its metallic threads and panniers that push the skirt out to the sides, has a symbolic courtly purpose.

    D. A coat from 1833, with its faux waist and lengthened trousers, provides a sense of elegance and height to the man wearing it.

    E. In the mid-19th century, there was a desire to have skirts (generated by the Paris fashion) that were as large as possible.

        1. Women wore a slip, then an enormous whalebone and wood contraption that supported acres of fabric and a long train.

        2. The military braiding along the top and sides of an American dress from 1855–1865 suggests that it may have been made during or immediately after the Civil War.

F. A fancy dress was designed by Paul Poiret in 1911 for an elaborate party in which everyone dressed as if they came from an *Arabian Nights* tale.

G. Caroline Reboux was one of the great French designers who made simple, elegant clothes. Toward the end of her life, she created modern costumes like a 1920s cape which combined unprecedented designs with a sense of antique fashion from the Old Testament.

H. The museum has great collections of work by Coco Chanel, the most famous fashion designer of the first half of the 20th century.

   1. Her coat (c. 1927) falls like a Grecian costume, creating a sense in which costumes are not structured anymore (like Reboux's work).

   2. Chanel's most famous design is her 1938 business suit; its modesty suggests that the wearer is not meant to be an object of sexual desire.

I. The shoe collection at The Metropolitan Museum of Art contains thousands of fascinating shoes. Salvatore Ferragamo's sandals (1938), with their colorful layers of pillowed leather, remind one of late-1960s fashion.

J. "*L'Eléphant Blanc*" (spring/summer 1958) by Yves Saint Laurent—which shimmers as one walks—and *Ensemble* (1967) by Rudy Gernreich—with its strips of fabric and exposed flesh—look like nothing in the pervious history of art.

K. In *I Love New York* (2000), Miguel Adrover combines the two things New York City does so well: street art and incredible refinement.

III. The Antonio Ratti Textile Center was established in 1995 and represents a great need on the part of The Metropolitan Museum of Art.

   A. The original problem with the textile collection at The Metropolitan Museum of Art was that no one was in charge of it; none of the curators in individual departments with textiles knew how to conserve them.

   B. In 1995, the museum established the Antonio Ratti Textile Center to keep, catalogue, conserve, document, photograph, and make whole the textiles from all departments.

   C. A sheet of royal linen from c. 1466 B.C. is one of the most ancient pieces of surviving textile.

1. It is very difficult to find ancient textiles except in dry places (such as Egypt).
2. Though unadorned and simple, the linen is so fine that it would be impossible to make today.

D. The Peruvian mantle from the 2nd or 1st century B.C. is both woven and crocheted (to bring out the feline masks). For the mantle's complex techniques to be understood, the Ratti Textile Center had to use a computer.

E. The museum has very rare early textiles. It is fascinating to look at textiles that survive as long as paintings on panel or sculptures made of immutable material.
1. The linen fragment from the late 3rd or 4th century is a Coptic fragment probably produced for funerary purposes; it is in perfect condition.
2. The fragment of printed Islamic textile from the 10th or 11th century was also probably a funerary fabric; the piece's block prints of lions project a power that we have seen in the arts of the ancient Near East.

F. An imperial textile made between 1330 and 1332 in China is made of silk but has gilded paper woven in to represent clouds.
1. There is no Chinese textile that survives in any collection in the world that is of this quality and date.
2. The piece, like other old textiles, is almost never shown because it is light sensitive.

G. A beautiful length of Venetian velvet was woven in the late 15th century by a series of craftsmen who learned their craft from the Ottoman Empire. An almost identical piece of velvet, woven in the same time period, can be found painted by Raphael in *Madonna and Child*.

Recommended Reading:

Druesedow. "Celebrating Fifty Years of the Costume Institute."

Stauffer, Hill, Evans, and Walker. *Textiles of Late Antiquity.*

Questions to Consider:

1. Choose your favorite costume item presented in this session. What attracts you to it and what is "art worthy" about this piece?

2. The museum's textiles have been collected from a diverse selection of cultures. How have textiles influenced other art forms (e.g., painting, sculpture) in these cultures?

Lecture Eighteen
American Art—1650–1865

Scope: At a time when Americans felt culturally inferior to Europeans, The Metropolitan Museum of Art was among the earliest American art museums to both devote whole galleries and acquisition funds to American art and seek out gifts of entire collections of American art. Unlike American art collections in Boston and Philadelphia, The Metropolitan Museum of Art's collections have always sought to be national rather than regional in scope—they do not even give particular attention to the achievement of New York-based artists and artisans. The first of two lectures will survey the painting, sculpture, and decorative arts produced in America from the 17th century through the end of the Civil War in 1865. These works include iconic paintings like Emanuel Leutze's *Washington Crossing the Delaware* (1851) and Gilbert Stuart's 1795 portrait of George Washington, as well as masterpieces by artists like John Singleton Copley and Thomas Cole. The lecture also explores the museum's offering of superb examples by America's first internationally significant artists, the Hudson River School. These paintings will be placed in the context of "folk" or "self-taught" artists like Ralph Earl and Edward Hicks and will be treated in terms of the oscillation between London and Paris as artistic models for American production. The lecture also will consider the development of American interiors, furniture, and decorative arts during the same period.

Outline

I. The ideology of The Metropolitan Museum of Art was to inspire artists and create a condition to improve and make more international the American art movement that began in the 18th century.

   A. By the end of the 19th century there was a desire on the part of certain American collectors to look at the origins of American art.

   B. The Metropolitan Museum of Art was one of the first museums to go back and collect 17th- and 18th-century American art and to form a portrait of American art that included painting, sculpture, furniture, ceramics, silver, and textiles.

    C. I am going to give two lectures dealing with the museum's collection of American art.

        1. The first lecture will deal with the arts up to the Civil War.

        2. The second lecture will deal with the arts up to the 20th century and the development of the museum's Department of 20th Century Art [Department of Modern Art].

II. We are first going to look at a series of period rooms.

    A. The greatest rooms produced in America were collected by the museum very early and put into the American Wing in the mid-1920s, which set the standard for all displays of American art in American institutions.

    B. The Hart Room (1680) is a post-and-beam construction and contains works of furniture, including a bed, that were original to the room and part of an American idea of provincial English comfort. Had the room been European, the museum would never have collected it; the feeling on the part of the museum, however, was that Americans needed to understand where they came from and how they defined their styles.

    C. The 18th-century Marmion Room from King George County, Virginia, is a cabinet in space that reminds us of the most sophisticated rooms in the European galleries produced in England and France.

    D. In the Verplanck Room (1767), from a country house off the Hudson River, you can see that we are looking at a family with very English tastes. They are not hard-working American farmers but people of means like the provincial aristocracy in England.

    E. The Metropolitan Museum of Art does not think of itself as being only about New York.

        1. The museum is very interested in Southern decorative arts, such as the Richmond Room (1810).

        2. One sees in the room's French origins a combination of English and French Neoclassical taste—already, American rooms were at an international level.

III. The Metropolitan Museum of Art's collection of decorative arts is superb. Four objects give a sense of the range of material and illustrate the fact that the museum is not afraid to collect material that does not look sophisticated.

A. A turned chair from 1640–1680 is technically simple but possesses a level of provinciality.

B. A high chest of drawers ("highboy") from 1762–1775 has always been known as the "Madame de Pompadour highboy" due to the bust at the top that has always been thought to represent the official mistress of Louis XV. The object was made in Philadelphia before the American Revolution and tells you a lot about the wealth and sophistication of the American colonies.

C. The museum's collection of silver is huge; some of it can be seen in the period rooms and some can be seen in other cases (such as a silver teapot designed by Paul Revere, Jr. in 1782, which looks as if it could have been made in London).

D. The museum also has terrific collections of work by folk artists, including a sugar bowl made by Rudolph Christ (1789–1821) that is deeply inventive and tells us about taste and style outside of the metropolitan cities.

IV. The Metropolitan Museum of Art has a great collection of American paintings. Its collection is the broadest, and it is the least afraid of works of art that were collected and formed in Europe.

    A. American history paintings are not that common; we are more obsessed with describing our landscape and our people than we are with painting our history.

        1. The museum has the largest and most famous American history painting: Emanuel Leutze's *Washington Crossing the Delaware* (1851). The work has always been popular in America and endows George Washington with a sense of divinity.

        2. John Trumbull painted numerous history paintings, including *The Sortie Made by the Garrison of Gibraltar* (1789), which uses figural poses from Roman sarcophagi and Christian paintings.

    B. Matthew Pratt's *The American School* (1765) depicts the school of Benjamin West, the American painter who succeeded Sir Joshua Reynolds as the president of the Royal Academy in London. When this painting was made, there was no art school in America; artists went to Europe to learn how to make works of art.

    C. One of the largest works of art in the museum is John Vanderlyn's *The Palace and Gardens of Versailles* (1818–1819), a giant panorama meant to educate Americans about the grandeur of Versailles.

D. The museum has wonderful examples of paintings of great American heroes.

    1. The museum bought Charles Willson Peale's 1779–1781 painting of George Washington from the president's descendents in 1897.

    2. There are more than 18 versions of Gilbert Stuart's portrait of George Washington (begun in 1795), but the museum is convinced that its version is one that was painted (at least in part) from life.

    3. *Daniel Crommelin Verplanck* (1771) was painted by John Singleton Copley, the great portrait painter of Boston.

    4. There is also a strand of American portraiture that deals with ordinary people, such as Ralph Earl's portrait of Elijah Boardman from 1789, which communicates the idea of the self-made man.

E. *Still Life: Balsam Apple and Vegetables* (c. 1820s) is one of James Peale's most charming still lifes. The painting is flat and the composition is uninteresting, yet it is one of the best American still lifes from the 1820s.

F. *The Falls of Niagara* (c. 1825) by Edward Hicks addresses the American idea of manifest destiny. Manifest destiny and its pictorial embodiment are expressed in three other paintings in the museum.

    1. Thomas Cole's *View from Mount Holyoke, Northampton, Massachusetts, after a Thunderstorm—The Oxbow* (1836) looks down into the Connecticut Valley and sets a standard for American painting that was met by two other artists.

    2. Frederic Edwin Church's *Heart of the Andes* (1859) depicts a place of such majesty and beauty that one wants to go there immediately; there is the sense that America, by painting the whole hemisphere, in some way owns it.

    3. Albert Bierstadt's *The Rocky Mountains, Lander's Peak* (1863), shows us a mythic ideal of America before Europeans arrived.

Recommended Reading:

Caldwell, Roque, Johnson, and Luhrs. *American Paintings in The Metropolitan Museum of Art, Vol. 1.*

Gardner and Feld. *American Paintings: Catalogue of the Collection of the Metropolitan Museum of Art I: Painters Born by 1815.*

Roque. *The United States of America (The Metropolitan Museum of Art Series).*

Questions to Consider:

1. Should folk art and art by self-taught artists be included in the museum's collection? Why or why not?

2. Who is your favorite pre-Civil War American artist that is represented in the museum's collection and why?

Lecture Nineteen
American Art—1865–1900

Scope: The Metropolitan Museum of Art had a huge impact on the production and reception of art in New York City. As a result, the museum's collections of American painting, sculpture, and decorative arts from the last three decades of the 19th century are greater than those from the previous three centuries. Although American artists continued to flock to London, Paris, Rome, and Munich for their artistic training, numerous independent art schools and professional art academies opened in the United States—from New York to Cincinnati and St. Louis to California. Artists like Whistler, Cassatt, and Sargent—who spent most of their professional lives in Europe—or artists such as Homer, Eakins, and Chase—who, while aware of European trends, worked in America—were of an unparalleled cosmopolitanism; their works are exhibited in major European capitals as well as throughout America. The art scene in late 19th-century America, when considered in terms of its decorative arts (by firms like the Tiffany Company and the Herter Brothers) and sculpture (by Augustus Saint-Gaudens and Daniel Chester French), rivaled that of any traditional European capital.

Outline

I. All of the works of art we looked at in the last lecture were made before the Civil War. In this lecture, I want to turn to the years after the Civil War.

   A. By the 1870s, Americans began to make up for lost time and take up cultural production.

   B. Eastman Johnson's *The Hatch Family* (1870–1871) embodies the success, materialism, calm, and multi-generational nature of a country that put the war behind it. One can see that the New York of this era was clearly the richest city in America.

   C. We are going to see, as we go through The Metropolitan Museum of Art, the embodiment of that money in works of decorative arts, sculpture, and painting.

II. American furniture of the 1870s, 1880s, and 1890s is extraordinary.

A. Alexander Roux's cabinet, made around 1866, embodies a level of craftsmanship as high as any European cabinetmaker. It is a work of art invented for a new, optimistic American wealth that was deeply sophisticated and knew about Europe but did not need to copy a particular style or source.

B. A library table from 1882 by the Herter Brothers was made for William H. Vanderbilt's Fifth Avenue mansion.

   1. The table depicts both hemispheres and illustrates Vanderbilt's global empire.

   2. One can visit the Department of European Sculpture and Decorative Arts and find equally vulgar and equally grand furniture but nothing that looks quite like this piece.

C. Augustus Saint-Gaudens designed a fireplace for the entrance hall of Cornelius Vanderbilt's mansion (William H. Vanderbilt's son) between 1881 and 1883.

   1. The mosaic at the top contains an involved inscription in Latin, indicating that the family was well educated.

   2. The fireplace is about the power of money to impress; it also reflects an interfamily competition.

D. The loggia from Louis Comfort Tiffany's Laurelton Hall (c. 1905) has references from all over the world; the loggia's design was taken from a palace near Agra in India.

III. American sculptors in the same period of time also were accomplished. I want to discuss works by two sculptors.

   A. The first sculptor is Augustus Saint-Gaudens, who designed the Vanderbilt fireplace.

   1. *Hiawatha* (modeled 1871–1872; carved 1874) was made in Rome, the fountainhead of all Western sculpture.

   2. The source of the sculpture is *The Song of Hiawatha*, the 1855 epic poem by Henry Wadsworth Longfellow.

   3. The object is deeply ambivalent in its relationship between the Indian and the white man; it raised questions about the true meaning of America because it acknowledged the fact that there were Native Americans before there were Europeans.

   4. Saint-Gaudens also sculpted *Diana* (1893–1894), the weather vane on top of what was to be Madison Square Garden. The museum owns a two-foot gilded cast of this figure, made in or after 1894.

B. Saint-Gaudens's major rival was Daniel Chester French.

    1. He is known for *Alma Mater*, which stands outside Columbia University, and the statue of Lincoln in the Lincoln Memorial.

    2. *The Angel of Death and the Sculptor* from the *Milmore Memorial* (1889–1893; the museum's version, 1926) is a funerary monument that reminds one about the museum's mission to inspire artists.

IV. The paintings of this period in The Metropolitan Museum of Art comprise a definitive collection of American painting.

  A. *The Champion Single Sculls (Max Schmitt in a Single Scull)* from 1871 is by Thomas Eakins, the first American painter who could be shown alongside any European artist.

    1. Eakins studied with Gérôme, one of Paris's great Orientalist painters; thus, there is a transference of the highest level of French academic painting to Philadelphia in the early 1870s.

    2. Most of Eakins's paintings are in the Philadelphia Museum but this work is in The Metropolitan Museum of Art— illustrating that the museum wants to take on the nation with its collection.

  B. Mary Cassatt joined the Impressionists in the Impressionist exhibition of 1879.

    1. She did not disguise her gender, unlike other female artists who were afraid their paintings would not sell because they were women.

    2. *The Cup of Tea* (c. 1880–1881) was shown at the Impressionist exhibition of 1881.

    3. The painting's subject, Cassatt's sister Lydia, is a model for the wealthy, fashionable young American woman in Paris.

  C. The single most controversial painting in The Metropolitan Museum of Art is John Singer Sargent's *Madame X (Madame Pierre Gautreau)* from 1883–1884.

    1. Madame Pierre Gautreau was one of the most scandalous women in Paris; in the 1880s, her revealing dress was considered shocking.

    2. When the painting was first shown, the shoulder strap of the dress was on her arm, implying that the dress could just tumble off.

  D. James McNeill Whistler, like Sargent, spent almost no time in the United States, though he had American patrons.

1. *Arrangement in Flesh Colour and Black: Portrait of Theodore Duret* (1883) is one of his great portraits of New York and represents one of the most important French art critics.
2. The portrait has a quality of international élan that only Whistler could capture during this period of time.

E. *Arques-la-Bataille* (1885) by John Henry Twachtman is concerned with tones of color. Its aesthetic comes from Japanese paintings, screen paintings, and prints. The museum also owns a small-scale study painted at the site, as well as the larger picture painted in his Paris studio.

F. I want to show two paintings by the stars of the American Impressionist movement.
   1. In Childe Hassam's *Celia Thaxter's Garden, Isles of Shoals, Maine* (1890), one can see the artist applying a European idea of art to the United States.
   2. William Merritt Chase's *At the Seaside* (c. 1892), like Hassam's piece, was painted out of doors (instead of from a sketch) so that the natural light saturation affected the way he saw nature.

G. Winslow Homer's *The Gulf Stream* (1899) is an intensely painted seascape depicting the ocean as something not benign but terrifying.

Recommended Reading:

Luhrs, ed. *American Paintings in the Metropolitan Museum of Art.*

Salinger. *Masterpieces of American Painting in the Metropolitan Museum of Art.*

Questions to Consider:

1. How did the art produced in America from 1865 to 1900 rival European art traditions?

2. What role did New York City play in the development of American art from 1865 to 1900? What work of art in the museum sustains your conclusions?

Lecture Twenty
20th-Century Art—Before World War II

Scope: After the founding of the Museum of Modern Art in 1929, The Metropolitan Museum of Art collected mostly contemporary American art and waited for the works in the Museum of Modern Art to become sufficiently "old" enough to be transferred to its galleries (as stated in the Museum of Modern Art's charter). Because this rarely happened, The Metropolitan Museum of Art was forced to create its own Department of Contemporary Art in 1967, which was incorporated into the Department of 20th Century Art three years later; in 1987, the collection was given large galleries in the Lila Acheson Wallace Wing. The first of two lectures will deal with the superb holdings of painting, sculpture, and decorative arts from the first half of the century, including masterpieces by members of the European vanguard such as Picasso and Matisse, as well as major Americans like Charles Demuth and Georgia O'Keeffe. The lecture will also deal with the small but superb group of sculptures from the first half of the century as well as with the developing collection of early Modernist furniture and decorative arts. The culmination of the lecture will be the living room from Frank Lloyd Wright's Little House, which, though housed in the American Wing, is firmly a part of the museum's collection of 20th-century art.

Outline

I. The Metropolitan Museum of Art was always interested and active in dealing with contemporary art.

 A. The museum collected the work of living artists from the moment it was founded.

 B. Early in the 20th century, it received a fund specifically for buying American contemporary art.

 C. The museum was interested in the relationship between what people were making now and what people had made in the past.

 D. In 1929, the Museum of Modern Art (along with the already-established Whitney Museum) took on responsibility for contemporary European and American art.

E. In 1946, the author Gertrude Stein willed her portrait made by Picasso to The Metropolitan Museum of Art because she did not want it to be seen only with 20th-century art.

F. With this and a collection gifted by Alfred Stieglitz, the museum decided to form the Department of 20th Century Art. The department does not differentiate from European and American artists because, in the view of the museum, they are of equal level and quality.

G. I am going to give two lectures on the Department of 20th Century Art, divided by the great war of the mid-20th century: World War II.

II. We are going to look in this lecture at works of art in the department made before World War II, starting with the work of Pablo Picasso.

    A. *Harlequin* (1901) reflects many of the museum's drawings and prints that represent one of the characters of the *Commedia dell'arte*. If this painting was in the Museum of Modern Art instead of The Metropolitan Museum of Art, one would not think about the long history before it.

        1. The subject looks off to the left in a melancholic gesture; other works in the museum, whose subjects' heads are weighted down on their hands, clearly reflect this gesture.

        2. The picture asks questions of everything that had been done in old centuries by taking a stock figure and imbuing it with real concerns and tragic sadness.

    B. Picasso's 1906 portrait of Gertrude Stein is one of the great portraits in the history of art.

        1. Stein has the quality of being self-absorbed and strong in a way that excludes the viewer.

        2. The painting was a confrontation of two of the most monumental egos of the 20th century.

        3. The influence of early Iberian sculpted heads, with their stylized facial features, is evident in Picasso's depiction of Stein.

        4. Picasso was also influenced by Ingres's 1832 portrait of Louis François Bertin.

    C. Later works by Picasso abound in the collection. There are certain pictures that fit in The Metropolitan Museum of Art better than they do at the Museum of Modern Art, such as *Girl Reading at a Table* (1934).

    1. The portrait has a sense of abstraction and compactness that reminds one of other representations of female muses in the museum's galleries.

    2. The picture has an Old Master quality, as if Picasso were remembering the art of the past.

    3. Florene Schoenborn, one of the great collectors of Modernist art, gave this piece to The Metropolitan Museum of Art instead of the Museum of Modern Art because she felt it reverberated throughout the centuries.

D. Henri Matisse was the great opposite of Picasso. He was the most important color painter in France after the Impressionists and Gauguin.

    1. He relaxes the lessons of Gauguin, making his paintings flatter and calmer.

    2. *Nasturtiums with the Painting "Dance"* (1912) is a painting about another Matisse painting from early 1909, *Dance (I)*, in the Museum of Modern Art.

    3. The second version of this painting is 1912's *Nasturtiums with "The Dance" (II)* in the Pushkin Museum in Moscow.

    4. These great works of art reverberate with other major works, just like Old Master paintings.

E. The most important Surrealist painter who took vision beyond the senses and painted what he dreamt or feared is Salvador Dalí. The quality of the bizarre in *The Accommodations of Desire* (1929) is seen in many points in the history of art.

F. One of the great things about going to the Department of 20th Century Art is that it makes one want to rush out and see pre-20th-century paintings that are in advance of these works.

III. The collection of 20th-century sculpture is equally important.

A. *Antigraceful* (1913; cast 1950–1951), by the Futurist sculptor Umberto Boccioni, is a portrait of the artist's mother.

    1. Futurists thought that all art before them had been obsessed with the past; they wanted to rearrange art and think about the future.

    2. The piece is a sort of four-dimensional object in which Boccioni sees his mother from various points of view; it looks like an African mask in motion.

B. Purity of form is reflected in *Bird in Space* (1923) by Constantin Brancusi.

    1. Cycladic sculptures were important to him.

    2. The museum's marble seated harp player and standing female figure are more typical of Cycladic art's absolute abstraction.

    3. *Bird in Space* is one of 18 bird forms in stone and bronze made throughout the 1920s; the forms are a representation not of a bird but of flight.

C. Gaston Lachaise's 1927 sculpture *Standing Woman (Elevation)* displays female proportions that one sees only in paintings by artists like Rubens and Titian. The notion of both the figure's enormous weight and its grace is something this sculpture conveys like no other sculpture in Western art.

IV. I want to turn to 20th-century paintings before World War II.

A. *The Figure 5 in Gold* (1928) by Charles Demuth is actually a portrait of William Carlos Williams. It is one of eight portraits which have no features of the individual but which accumulate qualities of that individual and embody them in paint.

B. Grant Wood's *The Midnight Ride of Paul Revere* (1931) comes from the Henry Wadsworth Longfellow poem, "The Midnight Ride of Paul Revere."

    1. The town is a generic American town and the rider is a generic rider, creating an American sense of identity.

    2. Wood thought more about early Italian painting than about contemporary art; thus, this work fits gloriously in the museum.

C. Georgia O'Keeffe's *Cow's Skull: Red, White, and Blue* (1931) is an image of America different from anything we have seen before.

D. Balthus's *The Mountain* (1936) reminds one of earlier depictions of the seasons by Millet and Bruegel; the artist's landscapes and figures have deep sources in the history of art.

V. I want to end with a look at the decorative arts during this period.

A. A 1904 washstand by Charles Rennie Mackintosh is a modern piece, unrelated to the past and without ornamentation.

B. Josef Hoffman's tea service from around 1910 is reduced to pure form.

C. An armchair designed by Ludwig Mies van der Rohe in 1927 only has antecedents in the Bentwood furniture designed in Vienna and Paris in the 1890s and looks like nothing from the past.

D. A room from Frank Lloyd Wright's Little House in Wayzata, Minnesota (1912–1914), makes one think of an ideal American place.

Recommended Reading:

Lieberman. *Painters in Paris: 1895–1950.*

Tinterow. *Modern Europe.*

Questions to Consider:

1. Why is the museum's collection of modern art so important?
2. Choose a work of modern art in the museum's collection and describe why it is important to you.

Lecture Twenty-One
20th-Century Art—After World War II

Scope: In 1969, The Metropolitan Museum of Art's "New York Painting
and Sculpture: 1940–1970" exhibition marked the first time in
which a great art museum took down its crown jewels of painting
to display contemporary art. After the exhibition, The Metropolitan
Museum of Art's holdings increased extraordinarily. The
museum's collections from the second half of the 20th century are
particularly strong in the work of the so-called New York School
of abstract painters, who came to dominate world art in the 1940s.
The museum owns major works by members of this informal
group, including Jackson Pollock, Mark Rothko, and Willem de
Kooning. Since the 1960s, The Metropolitan Museum of Art has
been committed to exhibitions of recent art; thus, the collection
contains major holdings in other regional trends in the history of
art (such as Pop art, Op art, and Postmodern art). Over time, The
Metropolitan Museum of Art's collection has become more
eclectic and more publicly accessible than the canonical collection
of post-World War II art at the Museum of Modern Art.

Outline

I.   In 1969, The Metropolitan Museum of Art held an exhibition titled
     "New York Painting and Sculpture: 1940–1970."

   A. The exhibit was curated by Henry Geldzahler, the curator of the
   Department of 20th-Century Art.

   B. He took down all the European paintings in the galleries and
   replaced them with works by artists who painted in New York,
   most of whom were still alive.

   C. The exhibition marked the first time in which a great art museum
   had taken down its crown jewels to put up contemporary art.

   D. The point of the exhibition was that New York City was now the
   art capital of the world. After 1969, the holdings of The
   Metropolitan Museum of Art increased extraordinarily as the world
   after World War II became as important as the ancient world.

II. We are now going to be dealing with the collection of art in the
     Department of 20th-Century Art made after World War II.

A. Some of the most powerful works of art made in the late 1940s were made by European artists who had lived through the war.

B. Alberto Giacometti was a Swiss artist who worked in France. *Three Men Walking (II)*, made in 1949, is a sculpture that raises questions being asked by the most profound writers and philosophers after the war (e.g., Jean-Paul Sartre and Samuel Beckett). The three skeletal figures reflect the combinative power of despair and hope that one felt so strongly after World War II.

C. The German artist Max Beckmann lived out the war in Amsterdam. During that time, he began to make a series of triptychs, one of which is *Beginning* (1949).

   1. We see a series of deeply disturbed childhood memories affected by psychoanalysis and all the pressures upon modern life that both world wars placed upon Beckmann.

   2. Beckman is the subject of the triptych, and there is an attempt at a heroic escape from this flawed childhood and an attempt to tell viewers about the problems of living after World War II.

D. When one looks at *Three Men Walking (II)* and *Beginning*, one is reminded of the African and Oceanic art galleries and the galleries of early Christian art, respectively. One thinks about religion and modernity when looking at these supremely difficult works of art.

III. We are now going to look at a sequence of major masterpieces of American postwar painting made by artists who worked in New York.

A. Clyfford Still's *1947-8-W-No.1 (PH-114)*, made in 1947, is a canvas that has been attacked with paint by an artist interested in the battles of colors (in this case, the battle between black and white). There is the sense that one is watching a drama with as much emotional intensity as any work but without a particular subject.

B. Many artists who became major members of the avant-garde in New York in the late 1940s and early 1950s were immigrants.

   1. Willem de Kooning was Dutch and became a major force in American painting by the late 1930s.

   2. *Attic* (1949) has a double meaning: the attic of a house and Attic in the sense of being from the Mediterranean.

   3. What de Kooning was interested in was the pictorial representation of energy, which can be seen in both The

Portonaccio Sarcophagus and Poussin's *The Abduction of the Sabine Women.*

C. Jackson Pollock's *Autumn Rhythm (Number 30)* from 1950 is another work of art about sheer pictorial energy.
   1. Pollock did not paint on an easel but dripped paint onto a canvas on the floor; he did this so often and with such skill that he became a great master of calligraphic painting.
   2. The Metropolitan Museum of Art has huge holdings of calligraphic painting.

D. Mark Rothko was one of the great colorists who reinvented color painting. *No. 13 (White, Red on Yellow)*, made in 1958, was given to the museum by his estate in recognition of the great 1969 exhibition.
   1. The piece is much more complicated that one first thinks.
   2. The work is so reduced that it washes away centuries of old color painting.

E. If Rothko's paintings are about subtlety, Ellsworth Kelly's paintings are hard and strong. *Blue Green Red* (1962–1963) looks as if it was made by a machine, even though it was painstakingly made by hand.

F. Roy Lichtenstein's *Stepping Out* (1978) illustrates the lack of constraints on artistic freedoms.
   1. The female figure is a Cubist play on Marilyn Monroe, and the male figure reflects figures in works by the French painter Fernand Léger (such as 1944's *The Three Musicians*).
   2. One sees the interplay between New York and France and between 1940s art and 1970s art.

G. There is no modern artist more about New York City than Andy Warhol, who observed the city as only an outsider can.
   1. He understood the importance of photography and the power of the image.
   2. In *Self-Portrait* (1986), he wears a wig and prints camouflage on the back of the image (referencing another artistic product that has to do with war).

H. James Rosenquist's *House of Fire* (1981) is a Surrealist painting of different consumer goods. The work is about advertising and is painted with an airbrush, as if Rosenquist were painting a billboard.

I. In 1969, The Metropolitan Museum of Art held an exhibition called "Harlem On My Mind," curated by sociologist Allon Schoener.

    1. The exhibit stressed the importance of one of the most thriving urban aesthetic laboratories in the world.

    2. Romare Bearden's *The Block* (1971) is a series of six panels that re-creates the urban life of Harlem.

J. Red Grooms's *Chance Encounter at 3 A.M.* (1984) reflects how important New York City is for the arts.

Recommended Reading:

Lieberman, Messinger, Rewald, and Sims. *20th Century Art Painting 1945–85: Selections from the Collection of the Metropolitan Museum of Art.*

Miller. *Modern Design in the Metropolitan Museum of Art, 1890–1990.*

Questions to Consider:

1. Describe some works in the museum that belong to the New York School. What makes them part of that school?

2. Who is your favorite post-World War II artist represented at the museum and what appeals to you most about his or her stylistic approach?

Lecture Twenty-Two
The Robert Lehman Collection—1400–1800

Scope: When the great financier Robert Lehman died in 1969, he left his entire collection of works of art (built by himself and his father, Philip Lehman) to The Metropolitan Museum of Art on the condition that it be shown on its own as a "museum with the museum." When the Lehman Wing opened in 1975, there was considerable controversy in the press about the donor's right to control "from the grave"; the collection, however, is so rich, varied, and important that it is more or less like having the Frick Collection at home at The Metropolitan Museum of Art. The Robert Lehman Collection is so diverse that its catalogue comprises more than 40 hefty volumes covering all media of European and decorative art from 1300–1950. The first of two lectures will deal with the collection's major masterpieces of Old Master painting, mostly purchased early in the century by Philip Lehman but with judicious additions made by Robert. Included will be paintings by Botticelli, Petrus Christus, El Greco, Rembrandt, and Canaletto, along with a select group of works from the graphic and decorative arts; the aim of discussing these and other works will be to link them with their counterparts in the regular galleries of The Metropolitan Museum of Art.

Outline

I. Robert Lehman (1891–1969) was an American financial titan who spent his life forming a collection large and important enough to have formed its own museum.

    A. Lehman was devoted to The Metropolitan Museum of Art and had been a trustee for years.

    B. He had been an enemy of the fate of J. P. Morgan's collection, which was split among the museum's various departments.

    C. Lehman decided to give his entire collection to The Metropolitan Museum of Art on the condition that it be kept together and shown more or less in its entirety in rooms largely based upon his family's townhouse on 54th Street in New York City.

D. The Lehman Wing is in the back of the building facing Central Park.

E. After his graduation from Yale, Lehman became the curator of his father's collection of Old Master pictures; by the time Lehman was 40 years old, he was one of the best art historians and connoisseurs in the world.

II. I am going to take you on a tour of the Old Master paintings and drawings in the Lehman Collection.

    A. The Lehman Collection has many works by great artists with other works in the museum.

    B. The Robert Lehman Foundation has prepared a definitive multi-volume catalog of the Lehman Collection.

    C. There is a kind of intimacy that develops between a scholar and works of art in the Lehman Collection, which operates as an entity of its own.

III. The Lehman Collection has many good works from the early Italian Renaissance because Lehman went to Yale (which has one of the greatest collections of Italian gold-ground painting) and collected with a very discerning and knowledgeable eye.

    A. Bernardo Daddi's *The Assumption of the Virgin* (c. 1340) is a fragment of an altarpiece hung low on the wall so one can study the extraordinary brushwork and execution that, in the original altarpiece, would have been too high up to see closely.

    B. There are a large number of panels by the Osservanza Master (which probably came from one big altarpiece) representing Saint Anthony Abbot at various points in his life. The Lehman Collection has *Saint Anthony the Abbot in the Wilderness* (c. 1435).

        1. The work almost looks like a Surrealist painting.

        2. The Lehmans bought this painting because there were two other panels from the same altarpiece at Yale, including Sano di Pietro's *Saint Anthony Abbot Tormented by Demons* (c. 1435).

    C. Giovanni di Paolo's *The Creation of the World and the Expulsion from Paradise* (1445) is part of a fantastic altarpiece, another fragment of which the museum has in its regular collection is *Paradise*.

D. Sandro Botticelli's *The Annunciation* (c. 1485) is a predella panel: one of the narrative panels that runs underneath the devotional image for a large altarpiece.

  1. In this work, Botticelli masters one-point perspective.

  2. The work rhymes with a painting of the same subject that Lehman knew during his time at Yale: Neroccio de' Landi's *Annunciation* (c. 1475–1480).

  3. Looking at Leonardo da Vinci's *Annunciation* (c. 1473–1475) done around the same time as the Botticelli painting, one can see how incrementally painting in Florence developed in the 1470s, 1480s, and 1490s.

E. The Lehman Collection has another Annunciation painting by Hans Memling, a northern artist: *The Annunciation* (1480–1489).

  1. There is a sense of domestic closure in this work different from Botticelli's painting.

  2. The oil paint results in a chromatic brilliance not found in Botticelli's egg-based tempera; Memling's understanding of perspective, however, is not as advanced as Botticelli's.

F. *A Goldsmith in His Shop, Possibly Saint Eligius* (1449) by Petrus Christus tells us a good deal about contemporary life in the 15th century, as the saint is shown in the history of the painter. This image was the most important prototype for Quentin Metsys's *The Moneylender and His Wife* (1514).

IV. Great artists abound in the Lehman Collection. The richness of The Metropolitan Museum of Art is so vast that one has to unfortunately focus on a few works.

  A. In El Greco's *Saint Jerome as Cardinal* (c. 1610–1614), one feels as if one is looking at an actual human being. El Greco is not making up a saint from his imagination but working from a model.

  B. There is a glorious portrait by Rembrandt of a rather strange man: *Portrait of Gérard de Lairesse* (1665).

  1. Rembrandt gives the subject a certain amount of gravitas beyond his years; we can see the artist is painting his own sense of mortality as he looks at this curly-headed young man.

  2. In the museum's upstairs galleries, one can see Rembrandt's self-portrait from 1660 and imagine what it must have been like for the elderly Rembrandt to confront the young Lairesse.

C. The museum owns a painting by Lairesse: *Apollo and Aurora* (1671). Here, Lairesse goes beyond Rembrandt and thinks more about Italian Classical art and the art of Poussin.

D. *Condesa de Altamira and Her Daughter, María Augustina* (1787–1788) is a full-scale portrait by Francisco de Goya y Lucientes.

    1. There is nothing else of luxury in the work, so one focuses only upon the subject and her relationship with her daughter.

    2. The work is a mix between a portrait and a representation of the Virgin and Christ Child.

    3. The subject was the mother of Don Manuel Osorio Manrique de Zuñiga, whose depiction by Goya can be found in the museum's European galleries.

V. Now let us take a look at the drawings in the Robert Lehman Collection.

    A. The collection has one of Dürer's great self-portrait drawings (*Self-portrait, Study of a Hand and a Pillow*), done almost exactly at the same time as *Self-Portrait with Sea-Holly* (1493) [also called *Self-Portrait or Portrait of the Artist Holding a Thistle*]. The drawing has a wonderful verso, *Six Pillows*, which represents a set of pillows and reminds one of the wonderful plumped pillows in northern paintings of the late 15th and early 16th centuries, such as Rogier van der Weyden's *The Annunciation* (c. 1435).

    B. Rembrandt van Rijn's sketch (c. 1635) after da Vinci's *The Last Supper* (1498) shows one great artist getting as close as he possibly can to another. He abandoned the subject—one of the few great subjects in the history of Christian art that Rembrandt did not paint.

    C. The Robert Lehman Collection has an important group of 18th-century Venetian drawings.

        1. Canaletto's *Warwick Castle: The East Front* (1752) is so carefully done that it served the artist as a preparatory drawing for his sequence of paintings about this castle, one of which is *Warwick Castle, East Front from the Courtyard* (1752).

        2. Domenico Tiepolo's *The Burial of Punchinello* (c. 1800) is part of a sequence of drawings about a character from the *Commedia dell'arte* that makes us remember his painting *A Dance in the Country* (c. 1755), which features a similar character.

VI. There are marvelous decorative arts in the Lehman Collection.

    A. One can look at faience, earthenware, jewelry, Renaissance furniture, and picture frames.

    B. Bernaert van Orley and Pieter de Pannemaker's *The Last Supper* (1520–1530) is an extraordinary tapestry that represents the Last Supper as held around a square table instead of a long presentational table as in Rembrandt's drawing a century later. The artist based his tapestry on *The Last Supper* (1510) from Dürer's sequence of prints called *The Large Passion*.

Recommended Reading:

Hindman, D'Ancona, Palladino, and Saffiotti. *The Robert Lehman Collection at the Metropolitan Museum of Art.*

Szabó. *The Robert Lehman Collection: A Guide.*

Questions to Consider:

1. Why was Robert Lehman so important to the history of the museum?

2. Choose a painting from the Lehman Collection created between 1400 and 1800 and describe why it is important to you.

Lecture Twenty-Three
The Robert Lehman Collection—1800–1960

Scope: The second of two lectures on The Metropolitan Museum of Art's Robert Lehman Collection will deal with the large and varied works of 19th- and 20th-century painting collected by Robert Lehman himself. Lehman was greatly affected by New York City's 1913 Armory Show, which exhibited more than 1,250 works of art by modern artists. As a result of the show, Lehman devoted his life to stressing the importance of modern art in the wake of Old Master paintings and drawings. This group of works encompasses both painting and the graphic arts and, like the works in the previous lecture, complements in every way the museum's permanent collections. This lecture will focus on particular masterpieces by Ingres, Matisse, Monet, Renoir, and Seurat. It will be complemented by a short discussion of some of the collection's masterful drawings by those same artists and others, such as Degas and von Menzel.

Outline

I.   In the spring of 1913 (when Robert Lehman graduated from Yale), New York City held the first, largest, and most important exhibition devoted to modern art in the city: the Armory Show.

   A. The show exhibited more than 1,250 works of art by 300 European and American modern artists, including Brancusi, Matisse, Duchamp, Monet, Gauguin, and van Gogh.

   B. The show clearly had an effect on Lehman, who was blown away by what he saw.

   C. As a result of visits to the Armory Show, Lehman devoted the rest of his life to grafting modern art onto the tree of Old Master paintings and drawings.

   D. In this lecture, we are going to see more of Robert Lehman's collection than the collection of his father, Philip.

II. We are going to head right on into major works of modern art in the Robert Lehman Collection.

A. The collection has one of the most important portraits in Ingres's entire career: *Princesse de Broglie* (1851–1853). The subject looks at us with an acceptance of our gaze, as if she were accustomed to being looked at. One can go into the museum's shop and find reproductions of almost everything in this painting.

B. Jean-Baptiste Camille Corot's *Diana and Actaeon* (1836) reflects the way in which the French landscape was brought into the Salon.

    1. The Greco-Roman subjects are set in a sylvan landscape; one of the interesting things about Corot's subject pictures is that the subjects are subjugated to the landscape.

    2. The balance between setting and figure is one of Corot's most important contributions to the history of art.

C. Robert Lehman's father, Philip, was interested in Barbizon School paintings of the Forest of Fontainebleau that were fashionable in late 19th-century New York City.

III. Both Philip and Robert Lehman were open to Impressionism and Postimpressionism, which make up an important part of the collection.

    A. Claude Monet's *Landscape at Zaandam* (1871–1872) is one of the great Monets in The Metropolitan Museum of Art. The museum has almost 30 paintings from Monet throughout his career.

    B. One of the greatest late Impressionist pictures in the United States is *Two Young Girls at the Piano* (1892), Pierre-Auguste Renoir's first official success.

        1. Renoir became the greatest figure painting of the Impressionists alongside his friend, Edgar Degas.

        2. While Degas's figures are rooted in the Classical tradition, Renoir's figures are rooted in the tradition of Rubens, Watteau, and Boucher.

        3. There are three versions of this composition; The Metropolitan Museum of Art's version is in the best condition and is the most perfectly preserved.

    C. At the Armory Show, Lehman was introduced to the painting of Henri Matisse. He realized that Matisse was important in the history of art with the creation of a new kind of color painting, Fauvism.

        1. Fauvist paintings were so vulgar and unrelated to the way we see that they were described as painted by people without culture and civilization (*fauve* means "beast" in French).

     2.   Despite its size, *Olive Trees at Collioure* (1906) represents a significant moment in the history of color painting.

D.   Matisse's friend, André Derain, painted *Houses of Parliament at Night* (1905–1906).

     1.   Derain takes lessons from Matisse's depictions of Collioure and applies them to London to create a chromatic symphony that makes it clear he had already seen Monet's 1903–1904 picture of the same subject, *The Houses of Parliament (Effect of Fog)*.

     2.   Monet's paintings of the Houses of Parliament are not as colorful as Derain's Fauvist picture; they push London toward a symphony of blues and greens.

E.   Lehman also loved Pierre Bonnard, who was a member of the group of artists called *Les Nabis* ("The Prophets").

     1.   These artists were interested in seeing within their own daily lives a chromatic world so intense that the ordinariness of life is made extraordinary.

     2.   *Before Dinner* (1924) is so chromatically extraordinary that the emotion comes from the interrelationships among colors.

F.   Balthus's *Nude Before a Mirror* (1955) represents a young woman who was the artist's muse.

     1.   The subject's pose and manner are so Classical that we know Balthus was familiar with the poses of Egyptian art.

     2.   In the museum's Egyptian galleries, one can find a similar hieratic pose in a work like the statue of an offering bearer from around 1985 B.C.

IV.   The Lehman Collection's works on paper are extraordinary.

A.   Ingres's *Study for "Raphael and the Fornarina"* (c. 1814) was made in preparation for an 1814 painting that is in the Fogg Art Museum. One sees in Raphael's *Madonna della Seggiola ("Madonna of the Chair")* from around 1516 that the Lehman drawing is much more like the head in this painting than in the study for *Raphael and the Fornarina*.

B.   Jean-François Millet's *Women Carrying Fagots* (c. 1858) made on blue-grey paper possesses a bone-chilling quality.

C.   Degas's study of a ballet dancer (c. 1873) was made on hot pink paper that has faded over time.

1. The ballerinas rearranging their clothing on the back of the drawing recall Degas's *A Woman Ironing* (1873).
2. The drawing also has another rhyme in Degas's *Two Dancers* (1873).

D. There are three wonderful drawings in the Lehman Collection by Adolph von Menzel, the greatest German artist of the second half of the 19th century. *Studies of a Young Woman* (1870 or 1879) is a sheet of two heads, one against the light and one facing the light.

E. The Lehman Collection has six drawings by Renoir. *Young Girl in a Blue Dress* (c. 1890) is a fresh and fantastic watercolor that makes one realize he was as great a draftsman as his friend and rival, Cézanne.

F. The subject of Georges Seurat's *Study for "Les Poseuses"* (1886) looks at the viewer hieratically, as if she were an ancient Greek kouros or a work of Egyptian sculpture.

G. In Odilon Redon's *Pegasus and Bellerophon* (c. 1888), the mythical horse seems more human than its rider and looks at the viewer with a wisdom reflected in works of Greco-Roman antiquity.

H. The lecture ends with Felix Vallotton's *Street Scene in Paris* (1895) because of all the places in which Robert Lehman felt at home, it was Paris.

Recommended Reading:

Brettell, Forster-Hahn, Robinson, and Tomlinson. *The Robert Lehman Collection at the Metropolitan Museum of Art, Volume IX: Nineteenth- and Twentieth-Century European Drawings.*

Hindman, D'Ancona, Palladino, and Saffiotti. *The Robert Lehman Collection at the Metropolitan Museum of Art.*

Questions to Consider:

1. What impact did the donation of the Lehman Collection have on the museum and its stature?

2. Choose a painting from the Lehman Collection created between 1800 and 1960 and describe why it is important to you.

Lecture Twenty-Four
The People of the Museum

Scope: Though The Metropolitan Museum of Art may be a veritable encyclopedia of art history, the museum—like all great museums—is only as strong and resilient as the curators who run it and the donors who provide it with magnificent works of art. As a conclusion to this course, we will look at the people behind the museum's success. We will consider the impact of the museum's many curators, from its first, Luigi Palma di Cesnola (1832–1904), to its most recent, Philippe de Montebello (b. 1936). While the museum's curators have defined the mission and goals of The Metropolitan Museum of Art, the museum's donors and benefactors—including historical giants like J. P. Morgan (1837–1913) and John D. Rockefeller (1839–1937)—have provided it with a bounty of rare and exciting works of art. The Metropolitan Museum of Art is an institution made by individuals, some of whom were successful financially and others who were successful in terms of their art expertise. Bringing together these two worlds creates an extraordinary museum; understanding their impact creates an equally extraordinary museum experience.

Outline

I. Throughout our journey through The Metropolitan Museum of Art, we have been into every single department. You now have a sense of the whole range of the collections at this extraordinary art museum.

    A. I want to give you a sense of the other people at the museum whose tastes are a bit forgotten because their works are scattered throughout the museum.

    B. The contents of The Metropolitan Museum of Art come, by and large, from donations by those who believe in the institution and its mission; oftentimes, visitors to the museum do not think about these donors.

II. The Metropolitan Museum of Art's directors manage the staff, hire people, control the museum, work for the trustees, and define the principles and future goals of the museum.

A. The museum has been fortunate to have a series of directors who have stayed for a long time, fostering a sense of trust in the institution.

B. The first director of the museum was Luigi Palma di Cesnola (1832–1904).

    1. He became a passionate archaeologist in Cyprus and formed a huge collection of art.

    2. In 1879, when the Louvre considered purchasing his collection, The Metropolitan Museum of Art immediately brought the collection to the United States and made di Cesnola the first director of the museum.

    3. He convinced the museum's trustees that they could collect original antiquities, not just plaster casts of works that were in European museums and at archeological sites.

C. Thomas Hoving (b. 1931) was director of the museum during the period when it attained its vast size.

    1. Everything he did was associated with publicity, and he put The Metropolitan Museum of Art on the map.

    2. One of his most famous acquisitions is Velazquez's *Juan de Pareja (born about 1610, died 1670)*; the acquisition of this painting in 1971 brought people to the galleries of European paintings.

D. Philippe de Montebello (b. 1936) has been the museum's director for the last 30 years.

    1. He has improved the quality of both the museum and its galleries (including the new gallery for Greek and Roman art) and has made a series of extraordinary acquisitions.

    2. One of these acquisitions is Duccio's *Madonna and Child*, which added to the superb group of early Italian panel paintings in the museum.

III. The Metropolitan Museum of Art's donors are an incredible group of people composed of many extraordinary individuals.

A. J. P. Morgan (1837–1913) was one of the greatest donors in the history of the museum; he was a trustee from 1903 until his death in 1913.

    1. He gave a lot to the museum, including Raphael's *Madonna and Child Enthroned with Saints*.

    2. His gift of period rooms, including the bedroom from the Sagredo Palace in Venice, changed the institution.

B. William Kissam Vanderbilt (1849–1920) gave numerous works to the museum, including Boucher's *The Toilet of Venus*, Sir Joshua Reynolds's *Captain George K. H.* Coussmaker (1759–1801), and Sir Thomas Gainsborough's *Mrs. Grace Dalrymple Elliott (1754?–1823)*.

C. Henry Osborne Havemeyer (1847–1907) and his second wife, Louisine Elder Havemeyer (1855–1929), bequeathed an extraordinary collection to the museum that included Whose Sleeves? (Tagasode) from the late 16th century; Hokusai's prints (including *The Great Wave at Kanagawa*); Rembrandt's *Portrait of a Woman* (1632); El Greco's *View of Toledo*; Ingres's *Joseph-Antoine Moltedo (born 1775)*; Manet's *Mademoiselle V... in the Costume of an Espada*; Cézanne's *Mont Sainte-Victoire and the Viaduct of the Arc River Valley* (1882–1885); and Degas's *The Dancing Class* (probably 1871).

D. John D. Rockefeller (1839–1937) gave in more strategic ways. He had the economic power and foresight to make important pieces such as the Mesopotamian relief panels possible for the museum.

E. Jules Semon Bache (1861–1944) gave Petrus Christus's Portrait of a Carthusian.

F. Nelson Rockefeller (1908–1979) owned the Museum of Primitive Art, which became The Metropolitan Museum of Art's Department of African, Oceanic, and Ancient American Art; the museum would be poor without his belief in these kinds of art, including the mid-19th-century shield from the Solomon Islands, the Edo pendant mask, and the Mayan mirror bearer.

G. Jayne Wrightsman gave Vermeer's *Study of a Young Woman* (probably 1665–1667) to the museum in memory of Theodore Rousseau, Jr., who was the curator of European paintings. Other gifts of hers include *Rubens, His Wife Helena Fourment (1614-1673), and Their Son Peter Paul (born 1637)* by Rubens; *Allegory of the Planets and Continents* by Giambattista Tiepolo; *A Dance in the Country* by Giovanni Domenico Tiepolo; and *Piazza San Marco* by Canaletto.

IV. The Metropolitan Museum of Art is an institution made by individuals, some of whom were successful financially, others who were successful in terms of their art expertise. Bringing together these two worlds creates an extraordinary museum.

V. All art is human; it is made by people for people. There are extraordinary lessons to be learned from works of art when you go to a museum, and this is what I hope has become clear to you as a result of these lectures.

   A. We have talked about the relationship between mothers and children throughout the history of art as seen in works like Berlinghiero's *Madonna and Child* and *Yashoda and Krishna*.

   B. We can look at babies in the history of art, such as the Olmec baby figure and Andrea della Robbia's *Virgin and Child*.

   C. We can see numerous repetitions of infants and little children— including the marble *stele* of a little girl or John Singleton Copley's *Daniel Crommelin Verplanck*—or young men who have made it in the world: Ralph Earl's *Elijah Boardman* or Bronzino's *Portrait of a Young Man*.

   D. We can see images of aging throughout the history of art in every culture, such as Rembrandt's *Self-Portrait* or the pre-Columbian seated figure. There is the sense that one can investigate the human understanding of the life cycle simply by going to a museum.

   E. One can go through the museum's various departments and find works of art that speak about the power of the sea or the abundance of the land, such as Ogata Korin's *Rough Waves* (1704–1709) or van Ruysdael's *Wheat Fields* (c. 1670).

   F. The museum offers a great place to gain both tolerance for and knowledge of world religion through objects like the altarpiece dedicated to Buddha Maitreya, Raphael's *Madonna and Child Enthroned with Saints*, or the mihrab from Isfahan.

   G. The Metropolitan Museum of Art is literally inexhaustible—for that reason one should visit it throughout one's life.

Recommended Reading:

Frelinghuysen and Cooney. *Splendid Legacy: The Havemeyer Collection.*

Moffett. *Impressionist and Post-Impressionist Paintings in the Metropolitan Museum of Art.*

Weitzenhoffer. *Havemeyers: Impressionism Comes to America.*

Questions to Consider:

1. Why are gifts and bequests so important to the development of a museum like The Metropolitan Museum of Art?

2. Describe how select works discussed throughout the course illustrate various stages of the human life cycle.

Works Discussed

Notes:

The format and content of the entries in the Works Discussed list and on screen may vary somewhat depending upon the requirements of the organization that supplied the image. The titles of these works appear as listed in museum catalogues and may vary slightly from titles as used by the professor during a particular lecture.

Artists' names are shown in bold in the following list. If no name is cited, the artist is unknown. Works are listed in the order in which they first appear in the course; if a particular work reappears in another lecture, it is not cited again. Unless otherwise noted, all works of art are located in The Metropolitan Museum of Art in New York City.

Lecture One

Robert Havell, Jr. *View of the Bay and City of New York from Weehawken.* 1840. Oil on canvas, 24 × 33" (61 × 83.3 cm).

Childe Hassam. *Spring Morning in the Heart of the City.* 1890, reworked 1895–1899. Oil on canvas, 18 × 20¾" (46 × 52.7 cm).

George Wesley Bellows. *Pennsylvania Station Excavation.* 1907–1908. Oil on canvas, 31½ × 38¼" (79.2 × 97.1 cm). Brooklyn Museum of Art, Brooklyn.

Samuel Halpert. *The Flatiron Building.* 1919. Oil on canvas, 40 × 34" (101.6 × 86.4 cm).

Edward Hopper. *The City.* 1927. Oil on canvas, 28 × 36" (71.1 × 91.4 cm). University of Arizona Museum of Art, Tucson.

George Copeland Ault. *From Brooklyn Heights.* 1925. Oil on canvas, 30 × 20" (76.2 × 50.8 cm). The Newark Museum, Newark.

John Marin. *Lower Manhattan from the River, Number 1.* 1921. Watercolor, charcoal, and pencil on paper, 21½ × 26½" (55.6 × 67.3 cm).

Florine Stettheimer. *Spring Sale at Bendel's.* 1921. Oil on canvas, 50 × 40" (127 × 101.6 cm). Philadelphia Museum of Art, Philadelphia.

Stuart Davis. *New York Mural.* 1932. Oil on canvas, 84 × 48" (213 × 122 cm) Norton Museum of Art, West Palm Beach.

William Glackens. *The Drive, Central Park.* c. 1905. Oil on canvas, 25 × 31" (64.5 × 81 cm). The Cleveland Museum of Art, Cleveland.

———. *May Day, Central Park.* c. 1905. Oil on canvas, 25 × 30¼" (63.8 × 76.8 cm). Fine Arts Museum of San Francisco, San Francisco.

———. *Central Park, Winter.* c. 1905. Oil on canvas, 25 × 30" (63.5 × 76.2 cm).

Maurice Prendergast. *Central Park.* c. 1914–1915. Oil on canvas, 20¾ × 27" (52.7 × 68.6 cm).

Frank Waller. *Interior View of the Metropolitan Museum of Art when in Fourteenth Street.* 1881. Oil on canvas, 24 × 20" (61 × 50.8 cm).

Lecture Two

Asiatic garland sarcophagus. Mid-Imperial, Severan period, Roman. A.D. 200–225. Marble. Gift of Abdo Debbas, 1870.

Marble seated harp player. Cycladic. c. 2800–2700 B.C. Marble, H (with harp) 11½" (29.21 cm).

Terracotta stirrup jar with octopus. Mycenaean. c. 1200–1100 B.C. Terracotta, H 10¼" (26 cm), Diameter 8½" (21.5 cm).

Marble statue of a kouros (youth). Archaic, Greek, Attic. c. 590–580 B.C. Naxian marble, H (without plinth) 78" (194.6 cm), H (of head) 12" (30.5 cm), L (of face) 9" (22.6 cm), W (of shoulders) 18" (51.6 cm).

Grave stele of a youth and a little girl with finial in the form of a sphinx. Archaic, Greek, Attic. c. 530 B.C. Marble, H 13'11" (423 cm).

Marble grave stele of a little girl. Classical Greek. c. 450–440 B.C. Parian marble, H 31½" (80 cm).

Exekias (attributed). Neck-amphora with lid. Archaic, Greek, Attic. c. 540 B.C. Terracotta, H 18½" (47 cm).

Andokides (potter), the Andokides Painter (red-figure decoration, attributed), and the Lysippides Painter (black-figure decoration, attributed). Amphora. Greek, Attic. c. 530 B.C. Terracotta, H 22¾" (57.5 cm).

Chariot with scenes from the life of the Greek hero Achilles. Etruscan, Archaic. Second quarter of the 6th century B.C. Bronze inlaid with ivory, H 51¾" (131.1 cm), L (of pole) 82" (209 cm).

The Ganymede Jewelry. Hellenistic, Greek. c. 330–300 B.C. Gold, rock crystal, emerald, L (of necklace) 13" (33 cm), H (of earrings) 2½" (6 cm), W (of bracelets) 3" (8 cm), W (of fibulae) 2" (5 cm), H (of ring) 1" (2.1 cm).

Cubiculum (bedroom) from the Villa of P. Fannius Synistor. Roman. c. 40–30 B.C. Fresco, Room 8'8½" × 10'11½ × 19'7" (265 × 334 x 583 cm).

Portrait statue of a boy. Roman. Late 1st century B.C.–A.D. early 1st century. Bronze, H 52" (132.4 cm), L (of face) 5" (13 cm).

Statue of the Emperor Trebonianus Gallus. Roman. A.D. 251–253. Bronze, H 96" (241 cm).

Funerary altar of Cominia Tyche. Roman, Imperial, Flavian, or Trajanic. c. A.D. 90–100. Marble, H 40".

Marble sarcophagus with the Triumph of Dionysos and the Seasons. Roman. c. A.D. 260–270. Phrygian marble, overall 36 × 84 × 36" (86 × 215 × 92 cm).

Lecture Three

Comb. Predynastic period, Egyptian. c. 3200 B.C. Ivory, H 2¼" (5.7 cm).

Statue of Memi and Sabu. Old Kingdom, Dynasty 4, Egyptian. c. 2575–2465 B.C. Painted limestone, H 24½" (62 cm).

Sphinx of Senwosret III. Middle Kingdom, Dynasty 12, Egyptian. c. 1878–1841 B.C. Gneiss, L 28¾" (73 cm).

Fragmentary Head of a Queen. New Kingdom, Dynasty 18, Egyptian. c. 1352–1336 B.C. Yellow jasper, H 5½" (14 cm).

Akhenaten Sacrificing a Duck. New Kingdom, Dynasty 18, Egyptian. c. 1353–1336 B.C. Limestone, H 9¾" (24.4 cm).

Magical Stela. Late Dynastic period, Dynasty 30, Egyptian. 360–343 B.C. Greywacke, H 33" (83.5 cm).

Model of a Riverboat. Middle Kingdom, Dynasty 12, Egyptian. c. 1985 B.C. Gessoed and painted wood, linen twine, linen, L 50½" (128.9 cm).

Ritual Figure. Middle Kingdom, Dynasty 12, Egyptian. c. 1929–1878 B.C. Plastered and painted cedar, H 23" (55.5 cm).

Coffin of Khnum-nakht. Middle Kingdom, Dynasty 12, Egyptian. c. 1900–1800 B.C. Painted wood, L 82" (208 cm).

Outer Coffin of Henettawy. Third Intermediate period, Dynasty 21, Egyptian. c. 1040–991 B.C. Plastered and painted wood, L 78" (203 cm).

Heart Scarab of Hatnofer. New Kingdom, Dynasty 18, Egyptian. c. 1466 B.C. Gold, green stone, 2¾ × 2¼" (6.7 × 5.3 cm).

Chair of Renyseneb. New Kingdom, mid-Dynasty 18, Egyptian. c. 1450 B.C. Ebony, ivory, H 35" (86.2 cm).

Sphinx of Amenhotep III. New Kingdom, Dynasty 18, Egyptian.
c. 1391–1353 B.C. Egyptian faience, L 10" (25 cm).

Cat. Ptolemaic period, Egyptian. 330–30 B.C. Bronze, H 11" (27.9 cm).

Tomb of Perneb. End of Dynasty 5, Old Kingdom, Egyptian.
c. 2350–2323 B.C. Limestone (partially painted), H 193" (482 cm).

The Temple of Dendur. Roman period, Egyptian. c. 15 B.C. Sandstone, L
(from gate to rear of temple) 82' (2460 cm).

Lecture Four

Standing Bodhisattva Maitreya, the Buddha of the Future. Kushan period,
Pakistan. c. 3rd century. Gray schist, H 60" (163.2 cm).

Shiva as Lord of Dance (Nataraja). Chola period, India. c. 11th century.
Copper alloy, H 27" (68.3 cm), D 22¼" (56.5 cm).

Loving Couple (Mithuna). Eastern Ganga dynasty, Orissa, India. 13th
century. Ferruginous stone, H 72" (182.9 cm).

Yashoda and Krishna. Vijayanagar period, India. c. early 14th century.
Copper alloy, H 13" (33.3 cm).

Altar Set. Early Western Chou period, China, late 11th century B.C.
Bronze, H (platform) 7" (18.1 cm), H (largest vessel) 18½" (47 cm).

Altarpiece Dedicated to Buddha Maitreya. Northern Wei dynasty, China.
A.D. 524. Gilt bronze, 30¼ × 16 × 9¾" (76.9 × 40.6 × 24.8 cm).

Seated Buddha. Tang dynasty, China. c. A.D. 650. Dry lacquer with traces
of gilt and polychrome pigments, H 38 × 27" (96.5 × 68.6 cm).

Qu Ding (attributed). *Summer Mountains.* Northern Song dynasty, China.
11th century. Ink and light color on silk, 17½ × 46" (44.1 × 116.8 cm).

Jar. Ming dynasty, Xuande mark and period (1426–1435), China. Porcelain
painted in underglaze blue, H 19" (48.3 cm).

Chuba. Qing dynasty, China. 17th century. Cut velvet with patterned wefts
of multicolored silks, gold-wrapped silk, and peacock-feather filaments, W
55" (139.7 cm).

Bust of Warrior. Kofun period, Japan. 5th–6th century. Earthenware with
painted, incised, and applied decoration, H 13 × 11" (33.3 × 27.6 cm).

Wisdom King Fudo (Fudo Myo-o). Heian period, Japan. 12th century.
Joined-woodblock construction with pigments, H 63¾" (162 cm).

The Battles of the Hôgen and Heiji. Edo period, Japan. 17th century. Ink,
color, and gold on paper, each 5' × 11'8" (154 × 355 cm).

Ogata Korin. *Rough Waves.* Edo period, Japan. c. 1704–1709. Ink, color, and gold on gilded paper, 57¾ × 65" (146.6 × 165.4 cm).

Katsushika Hokusai. *The Great Wave at Kanagawa (from a Series of Thirty-Six Views of Mount Fuji).* Edo period, Japan. c. 1830–1832. Ink and color on paper, 10 × 15" (25.7 × 37.9 cm).

Lecture Five

Storage jar decorated with mountain goats. Chalcolithic, Sialk III 7, Iran. 4th millennium B.C. Ceramic, paint, H 21" (53 cm).

Kneeling bull holding a spouted vessel. Proto-Elamite, Iran. 3100–2900 B.C. Silver, H 6" (16.3 cm).

Headdress, necklace, and hair ribbons. Early Dynastic IIIa, Mesopotamia, Ur. 2600–2500 B.C. Gold, lapis lazuli, carnelian, L 15¼" (38.5 cm).

Head of a ruler. Akkadian (?), Early Bronze Age, Iran or Mesopotamia. 2300–2000 B.C. Arsenical copper, H 13" (34.3 cm).

Human-headed winged bull and winged lion (lamassu). Neo-Assyrian period, Mesopotamia, Nimrud. 883–859 B.C. Alabaster (gypsum), H 10'3½" (313 cm).

Two panels with striding lions. Neo-Babylonian, Mesopotamia, Babylon. 604–562 B.C. Glazed brick, H 38¼" (97.2 cm).

Vessel terminating in the forepart of a fantastic leonine creature. Achaemenid, Iran. 5th century B.C. Gold, H 6¾" (17 cm).

Ewer with dancing females within arcades. Sasanian, Iran. 6th–7th century. Silver, mercury gilding, H 13" (34 cm).

Ewer. Umayyad period, Iran. 7th century. Bronze (cast, chased, and inlaid with copper), H 19" (48.5 cm), D (maximum) 8¼" (21.1 cm).

Bowl. Samanid period, Nishapur or Samarqand Iran (attributed). 10th century. Earthenware, white engobe, slip painted and incised under a transparent glaze, H 7" (17.8 cm), Diameter 18" (45.7 cm).

Plaque. Spanish Umayyad period, Cordoba, Spain (attributed). 10th–early 11th century. Ivory (carved and inlaid with quartz and pigment), 4¼ × 8" (10.8 × 20.3 cm).

Mihrab. Isfahan, Iran. A.D. 1354–1355/A.H. 755. Mosaic of monochrome glaze tiles on frit body, set into plaster, 11'3" × 9'6" (3.43 × 2.88 cm).

Carpet. Ottoman period, Bursa or Istanbul, Turkey (attributed). Late 16th century. Silk (warp and weft), wool (pile), cotton (pile), asymmetrically knotted pile, rug 66 × 48" (172.7 × 127 cm), storage box 99 × 42" (251 × 105 cm).

Qur'an manuscript. Nasrid period, Spain (attributed). 13th–14th century. Ink, colors, and gold on parchment, 21 × 22" (53.5 × 55.9 cm).

Abu'l Qasim Firdausi (author), Sultan Muhammad (artist, attributed). *Shahnama (The Book of Kings) of Shah Tahmasp.* Safavid period, Tabriz, Iran. c. 1520–1522. Colors, ink, silver, and gold on paper, painting 9½ × 9" (21.4 × 23 cm), entire page 18½ × 12¾" (47 × 32.1 cm).

Tughra of Sultan Sulaiman the Magnificent. Ottoman period, Istanbul, Turkey (attributed). 16th century. Ink, colors, and gold on paper, 20½ × 25½" (52.1 × 64.5 cm).

Nur al-Din Room. Ottoman period, Damascus, Syria (attibuted). A.D. 1707/A.H. 1119. Wood, marble, stucco, glass, mother-of-pearl, ceramics, tile, stone, iron, colors, gold, 264½ × 200½" (671 × 509 cm), D (from inside front entrance to back wall) 312¾" (804 cm).

Lecture Six

Berlinghiero. *Madonna and Child.* c. 1230. Tempera on panel, gold ground, overall 31¾ × 21" (80.3 × 53.7 cm), painted surface 30 × 19½" (76.2 × 49.5 cm).

Duccio di Buoninsegna. *Madonna and Child.* c. 1300. Tempera and gold on panel, overall (with engaged frame) 11 × 8¼" (27.9 × 21 cm), painted surface 9½ × 6½" (23.8 × 16.5 cm).

Giotto di Bondone. *The Epiphany.* Possibly c. 1320. Tempera on panel, gold ground, 17¾ × 17¼" (45.1 × 43.8 cm).

Simone Martini. *Saint Andrew.* Probably c. 1326. Tempera on panel, gold ground, 22½ × 15" (57.2 × 37.8 cm).

Sassetta. *The Journey of the Magi.* c. 1435. Tempera and gold on panel, 8½ × 11¾" (21.6 × 29.8 cm).

————. *Adoration of the Magi.* c. 1435. Tempera and gold on panel, overall 12¼ × 15" (31.1 × 38.3 cm), painted surface 12 × 14" (30.5 × 35.5 cm). Chigi-Saracini Collection, Siena.

Fra Angelico (attributed). *The Crucifixion.* c. 1420. Tempera on panel, gold ground, 25 × 19" (63.8 × 48.3 cm).

Jan van Eyck and Workshop Assistant. *The Crucifixion; The Last Judgment.* c. 1430. Oil on canvas, transferred from wood, each 22¼ × 7¾" (56.5 × 19.7 cm).

Andrea Mantegna. *The Adoration of the Shepherds.* Shortly after 1450. Tempera on canvas, transferred from wood, overall 15¾ × 22" (40 × 55.6 cm), painted surface 15 × 21" (37.8 × 53.3 cm).

Carlo Crivelli. *Pietà.* 1476. Tempera on panel, gold ground, overall 28¼ × 25½" (71.8 × 64.5 cm), painted surface 28 × 25" (71.1 × 63.8 cm).

Fra Filippo Lippi. *Portrait of a Woman with a Man at a Casement.* c. 1440. Tempera on panel, 25¼ × 16½" (64.1 × 41.9 cm).

Petrus Christus. *Portrait of a Carthusian.* 1446. Oil on panel, overall 11½ × 8½" (29.2 × 21.6 cm), painted surface 11½ × 7½" (29.2 × 18.7 cm).

Rogier van der Weyden. *Francesco d'Este* (*born around 1430, died after 1475*). c. 1460. Oil on panel, overall 12½ × 8¾" (31.8 × 22.2 cm), painted surface (each side) 11¾ × 8" (29.8 × 20.3 cm).

Hans Memling. *Tommaso di Folco Portinari* (*1428–1501*). Probably 1470. Overall 17½ × 13¼" (44.1 × 33.7 cm), painted surface 16¾ × 12½" (42.2 × 31.8 cm).

————. *Maria Portinari* (*Maria Maddalena Baroncelli, born 1456*). Probably 1470. Overall 17½ × 13½" (44.1 × 34 cm), painted surface 16¾ × 12¾" (42.2 × 32.1 cm).

Dieric Bouts. *Virgin and Child.* c. 1455–1460. Oil on panel, 8½ × 6½" (21.6 × 16.5 cm).

Giovanni Bellini. *Madonna and Child.* Probably late 1480s. Oil on panel, 35 × 28" (88.9 × 71.1 cm).

Sandro Botticelli. *Three Miracles of Saint Zenobius.* 1500–1510. Tempera on panel, 26½ × 59¼" (67.3 × 150.5 cm).

Piero di Cosimo (Piero di Lorenzo). *A Hunting Scene.* Tempera and oil transferred to masonite, 27¾ × 66¾" (70.5 × 169.5 cm).

Lecture Seven

Raphael. *Madonna and Child Enthroned with Saints.* c. 1504. Oil and gold on wood, main panel: overall 68 × 68" (172.4 × 172.4 cm), painted surface 66¾ × 66½" (169.5 × 168.9 cm); lunette: overall 29½ × 71" (74.9 × 180 cm), painted surface 25½ × 67½" (64.8 × 171.5 cm).

Albrecht Dürer. *Virgin and Child with Saint Anne.* Probably 1519. Oil on wood, 23¾ × 19¾" (60 × 49.8 cm).

Leonardo da Vinci. *Madonna and Child with Saint Anne.* c. 1510. Oil on panel, 65½ × 50¾" (168 × 130 cm). Musée du Louvre, Paris.

Hans Holbein the Younger. *Portrait of a Member of the Wedigh Family, Probably Hermann Wedigh (died 1560).* 1532. Oil on wood, 16¾ × 12¾" (42.2 × 32.4 cm), with added strip of ½" (1.3 cm) at bottom.

Bronzino. *Portrait of a Young Man.* 1530s. Oil on wood, 37¾ × 29½" (95.6 × 74.9 cm).

Titian and Workshop. *Venus and the Lute Player.* c. 1565–1570. Oil on canvas, 65 × 82½" (165 × 209 cm).

Caravaggio. *The Musicians.* c. 1595. Oil on canvas, 36¼ × 46¾" (92.1 × 118.4 cm).

Pieter Bruegel the Elder. *The Harvesters.* 1565. Oil on wood, overall (including added strips at top, bottom, and right) 47 × 63¾" (119 × 162 cm), original painted surface 46 × 63" (116.5 × 159.5 cm).

El Greco. *View of Toledo.* C. 1597–1599. Oil on canvas, 47¾ × 42¾" (121.3 × 108.6 cm).

Diego Rodríquez de Silva y Velázquez. *Portrait of Innocent* X. c. 1649. Oil on canvas, 55 X 45" (139.7 x 115 cm), Galleria Doria-Pamphili, Rome, Italy.
———. *Juan de Pareja (born about 1610, died 1670).* 1650. Oil on canvas, 32 × 27½" (81.3 × 69.9 cm).

Peter Paul Rubens. *Rubens, His Wife Helena Fourment (1614–1673), and Their Son Peter Paul (born 1637).* Probably late 1630s. Oil on wood, 80¼ × 62¼" (203 × 158 cm).

Nicolas Poussin. *The Abduction of the Sabine Women.* Probably 1633–1634. Oil on canvas, 61 × 82¾" (154 × 209 cm).

Rembrandt van Rijn. *Aristotle with a Bust of Homer.* 1653. Oil on canvas, 56½ × 53¾" (143.5 × 136.5 cm).

Hendrick ter Brugghen. *The Crucifixion with the Virgin and Saint John.* c. 1625. Oil on canvas, 61 × 40¼" (154.9 × 102.2 cm).

Johannes (Jan) Vermeer. *Allegory of the Catholic Faith.* c. 1670. Oil on canvas, 45 × 35" (114.3 × 88.9 cm).

Frans Hals. *Young Man and Woman in an Inn ("Yonker Ramp and His Sweetheart").* 1623. Oil on canvas, 41½ × 31¼" (105.4 × 79.4 cm).

Jacob Isaacksz van Ruisdael. *Wheat Fields.* c. 1670. Oil on canvas, 39½ × 51¼" (100 × 130.2 cm).

Lecture Eight

Sebastiano Ricci. *The Baptism of Christ.* c. early 18th century. Sketch, oil on canvas, 26 × 40" (66 × 101.6 cm).

Giovanni Battista Tiepolo. *The Triumph of Marius.* 1729. Oil on canvas, irregular painted surface, 18'4" × 10'8¾" (558 × 326 cm).

————. *Allegory of the Planets and Continents.* 1752. Oil on canvas, 73 × 55" (185.4 × 139.4 cm).

————. *Apollo and the Four Continents.* 1753. Fresco, 100 × 60'. Würzburg Residenz, Würzburg, Germany.

Giovanni Domenico Tiepolo. *A Dance in the Country.* c. 1755. Oil on canvas, 29¾ × 47¼" (75.6 × 120 cm).

Canaletto. *Piazza San Marco.* Possibly late 1720s. Oil on canvas, 27 × 44¼" (68.6 × 122.4 cm).

Francesco Guardi. *Fantastic Landscape.* Probably 1760s. Oil on canvas, irregular 61¼ × 74½" (155.6 × 189.2 cm).

Jean-Antoine Watteau. *Mezzetin.* Probably 1718–1720. Oil on canvas, 21¾ × 17" (55.2 × 43.2 cm).

Jean-Baptiste Siméon Chardin. *Soap Bubbles.* c. 1734. Oil on canvas, 24 × 25" (61 × 63.2 cm).

François Boucher. *The Toilet of Venus.* 1751. Oil on canvas, 42¾ × 33½" (108.3 × 85.1 cm).

Jean Baptiste Greuze. *Broken Eggs.* 1756 (submitted to the Salon of 1757). Oil on canvas, 28¾ × 37" (73 × 94 cm).

Jean Honoré Fragonard. *The Love Letter.* c. 1770. Oil on canvas, 32¾ × 26½" (83.2 × 67 cm).

Jacques-Louis David. *The Death of Socrates.* 1787. Oil on canvas, 51 × 77¼" (129.5 × 196.2 cm).

Sir Joshua Reynolds. *Captain George K. H. Coussmaker (1759–1801).* 1782. Oil on canvas, 93¾ × 57¼" (238 × 145 cm).

Thomas Gainsborough. *Mrs. Grace Dalrymple Elliott (1754?–1823).* 1778. Oil on canvas, 92¼ × 60½" (234 × 153 cm).

Sir Thomas Lawrence. *Elizabeth Farren (born about 1759, died 1829), Later Countess of Derby.* 1790. Oil on canvas, 94 × 57½" (238 × 146 cm).

Francisco de Goya y Lucientes. *Don Manuel Osorio Manrique de Zuñiga (1784–1792).* Possibly 1790s. Oil on canvas, 50 × 40" (127 × 101.6 cm).

Lecture Nine

Jean-Auguste-Dominique Ingres. *Joseph-Antoine Moltedo (born 1775).* c. 1810. Oil on canvas, 29¾ × 23" (75.2 × 58.1 cm).

Eugène Delacroix. *The Abduction of Rebecca.* 1846. Oil on canvas, 39½ × 32¼" (100.3 × 81.9 cm).

John Constable. *Salisbury Cathedral from the Bishop's Grounds.* c. 1825. Oil on canvas, 34¾ × 44" (87.9 × 111.8 cm).

Joseph Mallord William Turner. *Venice, from the Porch of the Madonna della Salute.* c. 1835. Oil on canvas, 36 × 48¼" (91.4 × 122.2 cm).

Jean-Baptiste Camille Corot. *Fontainebleau: Oak Trees at Bas-Bréau.* 1832 or 1833. Oil on paper, laid down on wood, 15¾ × 19½" (39.7 × 49.5 cm).

Pierre-Étienne-Théodore Rousseau. *The Forest in Winter at Sunset.* 1845–1867. Oil on canvas, 64 × 102½" (162 × 260 cm).

Jean-François Millet. *Haystacks: Autumn.* c. 1874. Oil on canvas, 33½ × 43½" (85.1 × 110.2 cm).

Gustave Courbet. *Young Women from the Village.* 1852. Oil on canvas, 76¾ × 102¾" (194 × 261 cm).

Édouard Manet. *Mademoiselle V... in the Costume of an Espada.* 1862. Oil on canvas, 65 × 50¼" (165.1 × 127.6 cm).

Camille Pissarro. *Jalais Hill, Pontoise.* 1867. Oil on canvas, 34¼ × 45¼" (87 × 114.9 cm).

Claude Monet. *Garden at Sainte-Adresse.* 1867. Oil on canvas, 38¾ × 51¼" (98.1 × 129.9 cm).

Édouard Manet. *Boating.* 1874. Oil on canvas, 38¼ × 51¼" (97.2 × 130.2 cm).

Pierre-Auguste Renoir. *Madame Georges Charpentier and Her Children.* 1878. Oil on canvas, 60½ × 75" (153.7 × 190.2 cm).

Edgar Degas. *At the Milliner's.* 1882. Pastel on pale gray wove paper, laid down on silk bolting, 30 × 34" (76.2 × 86.4 cm).

Georges-Pierre Seurat. *Circus Sideshow.* 1887–1888. Oil on canvas, 39¼ × 59" (99.7 × 149.9 cm).

Vincent van Gogh. *Sunflowers.* 1887. Oil on canvas, 17 × 24" (43.2 × 61 cm).

Paul Cézanne. *The Card Players.* 1890–1892. Oil on canvas, 25¾ × 32¼" (65.4 × 81.9 cm).

Paul Gauguin. *Ia Orana Maria (Hail Mary).* 1891. Oil on canvas, 44¾ × 34½" (113.7 × 87.6 cm).

Lecture Ten

Albrecht Dürer. *Samson Rending the Lion.* c. 1497–1498. Woodcut, sheet 16 × 12" (40.6 × 30.2 cm).

————. *Adam and Eve.* 1504. Engraving, 10 × 8" (25.1 × 20 cm).

Rembrandt van Rijn. *Christ Crucified between the Two Thieves: The Three Crosses.* 1653. Drypoint and engraving on vellum; first state of five, 15 × 17¼" (38.1 × 43.8 cm).

————. *Christ Crucified between the Two Thieves: The Three Crosses.* c. 1660. Drypoint, engraving, and scraping; fourth state of five.

Giovanni Battista Piranesi. *The Round Tower: Plate 3 of Carceri.* c. 1749–1750. Etching, engraving, sulphur tint or open bite, burnishing, 22 × 16½" (55.6 × 41.8 cm).

Francisco de Goya y Lucientes. *Picador Caught by a Bull (Bravo toro).* 1825. Lithograph, 12¼ × 1½" (31.1 × 41.6 cm).

Edgar Degas. *The Fireside.* c. 1876–1877. Monotype in black ink on white heavy laid paper, plate 16¾ × 23¼" (42.5 × 58.6 cm), sheet 19¾ × 25½" (50.2 × 64.8 cm).

Mary Cassatt. *Woman Bathing.* 1890–1891. Drypoint and aquatint (an etching process), printed in color, fourth state, plate 14½ × 10¾" (36.4 × 26.8 cm), sheet 17 × 11¾" (43.2 × 29.8 cm).

Leonardo da Vinci. *Head of the Virgin.* 1508–1512. Black chalk, red chalk, traces of white chalk (?), some remains of framing outline in pen and brown ink at upper right (not by Leonardo), 8 × 6¼" (20.3 × 15.6 cm).

Michelangelo Buonarroti. *Studies for the Libyan Sibyl (recto).* 1508–1512. Red chalk, sheet 11½ × 8½" (28.9 × 21.4 cm).

Giovanni Benedetto Castiglione. *Youth Playing a Pipe for a Satyr.* Date unknown. Brush with colored oil paint, paper partly saturated with oil, lined, 16 × 21¼" (40.6 × 53.5 cm).

Nicolas Poussin. *Bacchanal.* c. 1635–1636. Pen and brown ink, brush and brown wash over faint black chalk underdrawing, 5¼ × 8¼" (13.3 × 20.6 cm).

————. *The Triumph of Pan.* 1636. Oil on canvas, 53½ × 57½" (135.9 × 146 cm). The National Gallery, London.

Jean-Antoine Watteau. *Head of a Man.* c. 1718. Red and black chalk, 6 × 5¼" (14.9 × 13.1 cm).

Jean-Auguste-Dominique Ingres. *The Kaunitz Sisters (Leopoldine, Caroline, and Ferdinandine).* 1818. Graphite, 12 × 8¾" (30.1 × 22.2 cm).

Joseph Mallord William Turner. *The Lake of Zug.* 1843. Watercolor over graphite, 11¾ × 18½" (29.8 × 46.6 cm).

Lecture Eleven

William Henry Fox Talbot. *Leaf 8: Peony Leaf,* from: Album di Disegni Fotogenici, "The Bertoloni Album." Assembled 1839–1840. Page, 11 × 8½" (27.9 × 21.5 cm).

Albert Sands Southworth and Josiah Johnson Hawes. *Lemuel Shaw.* c. 1850. Daguerreotype, 8½ × 6½" (21.6 × 16.5 cm).

Gustave Le Gray. *Oak Tree and Rocks, Forest of Fontainebleau.* 1849–1852. Salted paper print from paper negative, 10 × 14¼" (25.2 × 35.7 cm).

Carleton E. Watkins. *View on the Columbia, Cascades.* 1867. Albumen silver print from glass negative, 15¾ × 20¾" (40 × 52.4 cm).

Nadar (Gaspard-Félix Tournachon). *Pierrot Laughing.* 1855. Gelatin-coated salted paper print (vernis-cuir), 10¾ × 8" (27.3 × 19.8 cm).

Louis-Rémy Robert. *Alfred Thompson Gobert.* 1849–1855. Salted paper print from paper negative, 9 × 6 ¾" (22.6 × 16.8 cm).

Julia Margaret Cameron. *Julia Jackson.* 1867. Albumen silver print from glass negative, 11 × 8¼" (27.4 × 20.6 cm).

Thomas Eakins. *Thomas Eakins and John Laurie Wallace at the Shore.* c. 1883. Platinum print, 10¼ × 8¼" (25.5 × 20.4 cm).

Edward Steichen. *The Flatiron.* 1904, printed 1909. Gum bichromate over platinum print, 19 × 15¼" (47.8 × 38.4 cm).

Alfred Stieglitz. *Georgia O'Keeffe.* 1918. Platinum print, 4¾ × 3¾" (11.7 × 9 cm).

Paul Strand. *Blind.* 1916. Platinum print, 13½ × 10¼" (34 × 25.7 cm).

Lewis W. Hine. *Steamfitter.* 1921. Gelatin silver print, 16¾ × 13" (42.1 × 30.9 cm).

Eugène Atget. *Shop front of "Courone d'or," Quai Bourbon.* 1922. Gelatin silver print, image 7 × 9" (17.7 × 22.4 cm).

Walker Evans. *Floyd and Lucille Burroughs on Porch, Hale County, Alabama.* 1936. Gelatin silver print, 7½ × 9½" (18.9 × 23.7 cm).

Man Ray. *Compass.* 1920. Gelatin silver print, 4¾ × 3½" (11.7 × 8.6 cm).

Garry Winogrand. *El Morocco.* 1955. Gelatin silver print, 9¼ × 13¼" (23.5 × 33.7 cm).

Lecture Twelve

Francesco di Giorgio Martini (designer), Guiliano da Maiano (executed by). *Studiolo* from the Ducal Palace in Gubbio, Italy. c. 1478–1482. Walnut, beech, rosewood, oak, and fruitwoods on walnut base, 15'11" × 16'12" × 12'7¼" (485 × 518 × 384 cm).

Abbondino Stazio of Massagno (probably stuccowork) and Carpoforo Mazzetti, probably after a model by Gasparo Diziani. Bedroom from the Sagredo Palace, Venice. c. 1718. Wood, stucco, marble, glass, 25'2" × 18'2" (767 × 553 cm), D 13'2" (401 cm).

David II Pfau (attributed to his pottery) and Hans Heinrich III Pfau (possible assistant). Tobias Stimmer and Christoph Murer (decoration after their designs). Stove. c. 1684–1685. Faience (tin-enameled earthenware), 10'4" × 6'10" (315 × 208 cm).

Paneling and chimneypiece from a room in a house on the Hall Quay, Great Yarmouth, Norfolk, England. c. 1600. Oak and stone, 114 × 24½ × 24½" (289 × 62 × 62 cm).

John Sanderson (designer). Dining Room from Kirtlington Park, Oxfordshire, England. 1748. Wood, plaster, marble, 36' × 24' × 20'3" (109 × 731 × 618 cm).

Robert Adam (designer). Tapestry Room from Croome Court. c. 1760–1769. Plaster, pine, mahogany, bronze-gilt, marble, lapis lazuli, steel, tapestry, 27'1" × 22'8" × 13'10" (825 × 690 × 423 cm).

————. The Lansdowne Dining Room from Lansdowne House, London. 1765–1768. Wood, plaster, and stone, 47' × 24'6" × 18' (143 × 746 × 548 cm).

The Cabris Room, *Boiserie* from the Hôtel de Cabris, Grasse. c. 1775–1778 and later. Oak and plaster (painted and gilded), bronze-gilt, mirror glass, oak flooring, etc., 306 × 120½ × 140½" (777 × 306 × 356 cm).

André-Charles Boulle. Commode. c. 1710–1732. Walnut veneered with ebony and marquetry of engraved brass and tortoiseshell, gilt-bronze mounts, verd antique marble top, 34½ × 50½ × 24¾" (87.6 × 128.3 × 62.9 cm).

Jean-Henri Riesener. Desk (Sécretaire). 1783. Oak veneered with ebony and Japanese lacquer, interiors veneered with tulipwood, amaranth, holly, and ebonized holly, gilt-bronze mounts, replaced velvet, marble tops, 57 × 43 × 16" (144.8 × 109.2 × 40.6 cm).

Charles-Guillaume Diehl (maker), Jean Brandely, and Emmanuel Fremiet (sculptors). Armoire. 1867. Oak veneered with cedar, walnut, ebony, and ivory; silvered-bronze mounts, 108 × 60 × 24" (238 × 151 × 60 cm).

Lecture Thirteen

Antonio Rossellino. *Madonna and Child with Angels.* 15th century. Marble, gilding on halo and dress, 28¾ × 20¼" (73 × 51.4 cm).

Andrea della Robbia. *Virgin and Child.* 15th century (c. 1470–1475). Glazed terracotta relief, 37¼ × 21¾" (94.9 × 54.9 cm).

Gian Lorenzo Bernini. *Bacchanal: A Faun Teased by Children.* c. 1616–1617. Marble, H 52" (132.1 cm).

Giovanni Battista Foggini. *Grand Prince Ferdinando de' Medici (1663–1713).* 17th century (c. 1683–1685). Marble, H (including base) 39" (99.1 cm).

————. *Cosimo III de' Medici, Grand Duke of Tuscany (1642–1723).* Marble, H (with base) 39".

Jean-Louis Lemoyne. *La Crainte des Traits de l'Amour (The Fear of the Arrows of Cupid).* 1739–1740. Marble, H 72" (182.9 cm).

Jean-Antoine Houdon. *Sabine Houdon.* 1788. White marble on gray marble base, overall (without base) 11 × 8½ × 6" (27.5 × 21.6 × 15.2 cm), H (with base) 13½" (44.5 cm).

Augustin Pajou. *Madame de Wailly.* 1789. Marble, base of gray marble, overall (without base) 24½ × 20½ × 10½" (62.2 × 52.1 × 26.7 cm), H (with base) 30¼" (76.8 cm).

Antonio Canova. *Perseus with the Head of Medusa.* 1804–1806. Marble, overall 92¼" (234 m). Fletcher Fund, 1967.

Apollo Belvedere. c. 350–320 B.C. Marble copy (Roman), H 88" (230 m). Museo Pio-Clementino, Vatican Museums, Vatican City.

Jean-Baptiste Carpeaux. *Ugolino and His Sons.* Modeled c. 1860–1861, executed in marble 1865–1867. Saint-Béat marble, H 78" (195.6 cm).

Edgar Degas. *The Little Fourteen-Year-Old Dancer.* Executed c. 1880, cast in 1922. Bronze, partially tinted, with cotton skirt and satin hair-ribbon, wood base, H (without base) 39" (99.1 cm).

Auguste Rodin. *Honoré de Balzac.* Probably 1891. Terracotta, H 9¼" (23.5 cm).

Lecture Fourteen

Feather Box. New Zealand, Maori. c. 18th century. Wood with shell inlay, 17¾" (44.7 cm).

Mask (Buk, krar, or kara). Australia, Torres Strait, Mabuiag Island. Mid- to late 19th century. Turtleshell, wood, feathers, coconut fiber, resin, shell, paint, 17½ × 25 × 22¾" (44.5 × 63.5 × 57.8 cm).

Standing Male Figure (Tiki). Mangareva (Gambier Islands), Mangarevan people. 18th–early 19th century. Wood, 38¾ × 10 × 7½" (98.4 × 25.4 × 19.1 cm).

Male Figure (Moai Tangata). Chile, Easter Island (Rapa Nui), Rapanui people. Early 19th century. Wood, obsidian, bone, 16 × 4 × 2½" (40.6 × 9.9 × 6.4 cm).

Shield (Grere'o [?]). Solomon Islands, possibly Santa Isabel Island. Early to mid-19th century. Cane, mother-of-pearl, pigments, fiber, 33¼ × 11 × 1½" (84.5 × 27.9 × 3.8 cm).

Helmet Mask (Temes Mbalmbal), Vanuatu, Malakula Island, Mbotgote. Mid-20th century, wood, vegetable fiber, pig tusks, glass, metal, paint, 26 × 15½ × 19" (66 × 39.4 × 48.3 cm).

Skull Hook (Agiba). Papua New Guinea, Kerewa, Pai'ia'a, Kikori Delta. 19th–early 20th century. Wood, paint, 56 × 29½ × 5" (142.2 × 74.9 × 12.7 cm).

Bis Poles. New Guinea, Irian Jaya, Faretsj River Asmat people, Omandesep. Mid-20th century. Wood, paint, fiber, 210 × 39 × 63" (538 × 99 × 16 cm).

Seated Figure. Mali, Djenné. 13th century. Terracotta, 10 × 11¾" (25.4 × 29.9 cm).

Pendant Mask. Iyoba, Nigeria, Edo, Court of Benin. 16th century. Ivory, iron, copper (?), 9½ × 5 × 3¼" (23.8 × 12.7 × 8.3 cm). Gift of Nelson A. Rockefeller, 1972.

Figure: Seated Couple. Mali, Dogon. 16th–19th century. Wood, metal, 28¾ × 9½" (73 × 23.7 cm).

The Buli Master (Ngongo ya Chintu possibly). Prestige Stool: Female Caryatid. Democratic Republic of Congo, Luba/Hemba. 19th century. Wood, metal studs, H 24" (61 cm).

Power Figure: Male (Nkisi). Democratic Republic of Congo, Kongo. 19th–20th century. Wood, pigment, nails, cloth, beads, shells, arrows, leather, nuts, twine, H 23 × 10¼ × 10" (58.8 × 26 × 25.4 cm).

Mask (Kpeliye). Côte d'Ivoire, Senufo. 19th–20th century. Wood, horns, fiber, cotton cloth, feather, metal, sacrificial material, 30¼ × 13 × 9" (76.8 × 33 × 22.9 cm).

Reliquary Head (Nlo Bieri). Gabon, Fang, Betsi group. 19th–20th century. Wood, metal, palm oil, 18½ × 9¾ × 6¾" (46.5 × 24.8 × 16.8 cm).

Lecture Fifteen

"Baby" Figure. Mexico, Olmec. 12th–9th century B.C. Ceramic, cinnabar, red ochre, H 13½ × 12½ × 5¾" (34 × 31.8 × 14.6 cm).

Mask. Mexico, Olmec. 10th–6th century B.C. Jadeite, H 6¾ × 6½ × 6½" (17.1 × 16 × 16 cm).

"Smiling" Figure. Mexico, Remojadas. 7th–8th century. Ceramic, 18¾ × 11¾ × 6¼" (47.5 × 29.9 × 15.9 cm).

Mirror-Bearer. Mexico or Guatemala, Maya. 6th century. Wood, red hematite traces, 14 × 9 × 9" (35.9 × 22.9 × 22.9 cm). Bequest of Nelson A. Rockefeller, 1979.

Vessel with Mythological Scene. Guatemala, Maya. 8th century. Ceramic, H 5½" (14 cm), Diameter 4½" (11.4 cm).

Seated Standard Bearer. Mexico, Aztec. Second half 15th–early 16th century. Laminated sandstone, H 31¾" (80.5 cm).

Frog Pendant. Costa Rica, Chiriquí. 11th–16th century. Cast gold, H 4" (10.5 cm).

Lime Container (*Popuro*). Colombia, Quimbaya. 1st–7th century. Cast gold, H 9" (22.9 cm).

Seated Figure. Colombia or Ecuador, Tolita/Tumaco. 1st century B.C.–A.D. 1st century. Ceramic, 25 × 14½ × 13" (63.5 × 36.8 × 33 cm).

Feline-Head Bottle. Peru, Tembladera. 9th–5th century B.C. Ceramic, postfired paint, H 12¾" (32.4 cm), W 8" (20.5 cm).

Feline Incense Vessel. Bolivia, Tiwanaku. 6th–9th century. Ceramic, H 10" (25.7 cm), W 8¼" (21 cm).

Double-spout bottle. Peru, Nazca. 2nd–4th century. Ceramic, H 6¼" (15.9 cm).

Funerary Mask. Peru, Sicán (Lambayeque). 10th–11th century. Gold, copper overlays, cinnabar, H 11½" (29.2 cm), W 19½" (49.5 cm).

Deer Vessel. Peru, Chimú. 14th–15th century. Silver (hammered), 5 × 3¼ × 7½" (12.7 × 8.3 × 19.1 cm).

Deity Figure (*Zemi*). Dominican Republic (?), Taino. 15th–16th century. Ironwood, shell, 27 × 8¾ × 9" (68.4 × 21.9 × 23.2 cm).

Dance Mask. Alaska, Yup'ik. Early 20th century. Wood, paint, feathers, H 24 × 23¾ × 6½" (61 × 60.3 × 16.5 cm).

Lecture Sixteen

Sallet. Italian. 1470–1480. Steel, copper-gilt, glass, polychromy, H 11¾" (30 cm), Weight 8 lb. 4 oz. (3.7 kg).

Burgonet with Falling Buffe. French. c. 1555. Steel, blued, and gilded, H 14" (35.5 cm), Weight 5 lb. 6 oz. (2.4 kg).

Justus Sustermans (Workshop). *Cosimo II de' Medici (1590–1621), Grand Duke of Tuscany.* Oil on canvas, transferred from wood, 78 × 48" (198.1 × 121.9 cm).

Armor of George Clifford, Third Earl of Cumberland. English. c. 1580–1585. Steel, etched, blued, and gilded, H 67" (176.5 cm), Weight 60 lb. (27.2 kg).

Lucas Cranach the Elder. *The Judgment of Paris.* Possibly c. 1528. Oil on panel, 40 × 28" (101.9 × 71.1 cm).

Armor (*Gusoku*). Edo period, Japanese. 16th and 18th century. Lacquered iron, mail, silk, copper-gilt, H 67" (176.5 cm).

James Morisset. Presentation Smallsword. English. 1798–1799. Silver-gilt, enamel, paste jewels, steel, L 41½" (105.4 cm), Weight 1 lb. 3 oz. (539 kg).

Saber. Ottoman period, Turkish. 19th century. Steel, jade, gold, assorted jewels, L 39¾" (100.97 cm).

Ambrosius Gemlich (etcher) and Peter Pech (maker). Double-Barreled Wheellock Pistol of Emperor Charles V. German. c. 1540–1545. Wood (cherry), steel, staghorn, L (overall) 19½" (49.2 cm), Weight 5 lb. 10 oz. (2551 gm), Caliber (each barrel) .46.

Samuel Colt (manufacturer) and Gustave Young (engraver). Colt Third Model Dragoon Percussion Revolver. American. c. 1853. Steel, gold, and walnut, L 14" (35.56 cm), L (barrel) 7½" (19.05 cm), Caliber .44.

Tournament Shield (*Targe*). German. c. 1450. Wood, H 22" (55.88 cm), W 16" (40.64 cm).

Girolamo da Treviso (attributed). Shield. Italian. c. 1535. Wood, Diameter 24¾" (62.53 cm).

Hans Ruckers the Elder. Double Virginal. Antwerp, Flanders. 1581. Wood, metal, L 19½" (49.5 cm), W 71¾" (182.2 cm).

Michele Todini. Harpsichord. Italian. c. 1675. Wood, various materials, inner instrument 106 × 34 × 7½" (269 × 87 × 19 cm).

Bartolomeo Cristofori. Grand Piano. Italian. 1720. Various materials, L (of case perpendicular to keyboard) 90" (228.6 cm), W (parallel to keyboard) 37½" (95.6 cm) D (of case without lid) 9" (23.5 cm), H (total) 34" (86.5 cm).

Matteo Sellas (attributed). Guitar. Italian. c. 1630–1650. Wood, bone, various materials, L 37¾" (96.5 cm).

Antonio Stradivari. Violin. Italian. 1693. Wood, L 23¼" (59 cm), W 7¾" (19.7 cm).

Mayuri (Peacock). Northern India. 19th century. Wood, parchment, metal, feathers, L 44" (112 cm).

Rag-Dung. Ming Dynasty, China. 1368–1644. Brass, copper, cloisonné, L 72" (188 cm), Diameter 12" (30.6 cm).

Sho. Early Tokugawa period, Japan. 19th century. Bamboo, wood, metal, L (longest pipe) 18" (45.4 cm), L (shortest pipe) 7" (18.1 cm).

Charles Joseph Sax. Clarinet in B-flat. Brussels, Belgium. 1830. Ivory, brass, L 26¾" (68 cm), L (of mouthpiece) 35" (89 cm), L (of barrel) 27½" (70 cm), L (of upper body section) 8¾" (22.1 cm), L (of lower body section) 10" (25.7 cm), L (of bell) 4¾" (11.8 cm), Diameter (of bell) 33½" (85 cm).

Bondjo. Democratic Republic of the Congo. c. 1915. Ivory, wood, polychrome, L 55" (139.5 cm), Diameter (greatest) 8¼" (20.8 cm).

Kodenji Hayashi (?). *O-daiko*. Tohshima?, Aichi Prefecture, Japan. c. 1873. Wood, metal, cloisonné kankodori, hide, silk, padding, H (of drum) 19" (48.3 cm), Diameter 22" (55.8 cm), H (of stand) 29" (73.7 cm), H (total) approximately 62" (approximately 158 cm), L (of drum) approximately 21" (approximately 53 cm), Diameter (of heads) approximately 17" (approximately 43 cm).

Lecture Seventeen

Doublet. French. Early 1620s. Silk, L (at center back) 19¾" (50.2 cm).

Shoes. French. 17th century. Silk, leather, L 10" (25.4 cm).

Court Dress. British. c. 1750. Silk, metallic thread, L (at center back): a. 49" (124.5 cm), b. 37" (94 cm); L (at c.) 11" (27.9 cm).

Coat. British. c. 1833. Silk, L (at center back) 38½" (97.8 cm).

Dress. American. 1855–1865. Silk, L (at center back): a. 30¾" (77.8 cm), b. 38¼" (97.2 cm), c. 59¼" (150.5 cm), d. 25" (63.5 cm).

Paul Poiret. Costume (Fancy Dress). 1911. Metal, silk, cotton, L 50¼" (127.6 cm), Diameter 8" (20.6 cm).

Caroline Reboux. Cape. 1920s. Silk, L (at center front) 47" (119.4 cm).

Gabrielle "Coco" Chanel (designer). Coat. c. 1927. Silk, metal, L (at center back) 44" (111.8 cm).

———. Suit. 1938. Silk, L (at center back): a. 22" (55.9 cm), b. 29" (73.7 cm).

Salvatore Ferragamo. Sandal. 1938. Leather, cork, 5½ × 9" (14 × 22.9 cm).

Yves Saint Laurent (designer). *"L'Eléphant Blanc."* Spring/summer 1958. Silk, metallic thread, glass, plastic, L (from shoulder to hem) 41¾" (106 cm).

Rudi Gernreich. *Ensemble.* 1967. Wool, plastic, nylon, L (at center back): a. 29" (74.5 cm), b. 8½" (22.5 cm), c. 22" (56.5 cm), d. 22" (56.5 cm), e. 23" (58.5 cm).

Miguel Adrover. *I Love New York.* 2000. Cotton, cotton/silk blend, synthetic, L (at center back) 27½" (69.9 cm).

Sheet of Royal Linen. Dynasty XVIII, Egyptian. c. 1466 B.C. Linen, W (greatest) 5'2" (161 cm), L (greatest) 16'11" (515 cm), Weight 2.9 oz. (140 g), 118 warp per square inch (46 warp per square cm), 77 weft per square inch (30 weft per square cm).

Mantle. Ocucaje, Peru. 2nd–1st century B.C. Camelid hair, 74 × 54" (118.9 × 137.8 cm).

Personification of Luna, the Moon, or Head of Diana, Goddess of the Hunt. Coptic period. Late 3rd–4th century. Linen, wool, 22 × 25" (56 × 63 cm).

Fragment with Printed Lions. Persian. 10th–11th century. Cotton and other fibers, 17¾ × 39" (45.1 × 99.1 cm).

Mandala. Yuan dynasty. c. 1330–1332. Silk, metallic thread, 96 × 82" (245 × 209 cm).

Length of Velvet. Italian. Late 15th century. Silk, metal thread, W 23" (58.4 cm), L 12'4" (375.9 cm).

Lecture Eighteen

The Hart Room. From the Thomas Hart House, in Ipswich, Massachusetts. 1680.

The Marmion Room. Small parlor from a plantation house in King George County, Virginia, home of the Fitzhugh family. 18th century. Walnut, pine, sienna marble and paint, 21' × 16'5" × 11' (6.42 × 5 × 3.32 m).

The Verplanck Room. Parlor from the Cadwallader Colden, Jr., house in Coldenham, New York. 1767.

The Richmond Room. Drawing Room from the Williams House, Richmond, Virginia. 1810.

Turned Armchair. 1640–1680. Ash, 44¾ × 23½ × 15¾" (113.7 × 59.7 × 40 cm).

Chest of drawers. c. 1762–1775. Mahogany, tulip poplar, yellow pine, 91 × 45 × 24" (233 × 113 × 62 cm).

Paul Revere, Jr. Teapot. c. 1782. Silver, overall 6½ × 9½" (16.5 × 23.8 cm), Weight 539.2 g (17.336 troy ounces), Diameter (of base) 4" (10.5 cm).

Rudolph Christ. Sugar Bowl. 1789–1821. Earthenware with slip decoration, 12¾" (32.4 cm), Diameter 10" (25.4 cm).

Emanuel Gottlieb Leutze. *Washington Crossing the Delaware*. 1851. Oil on canvas, 12'5" × 21'3" (378 × 647 cm).

John Trumbull. *The Sortie Made by the Garrison of Gibraltar*. 1789. Oil on canvas, 72 × 108" (180 × 271 cm).

Matthew Pratt. *The American School*. 1765. Oil on canvas, 36 × 50¼" (91.4 × 127.6 cm).

John Vanderlyn. *The Palace and Gardens of Versailles*. 1818–1819. Oil on canvas, 12 × 165' (365 × 5,029 cm).

Charles Willson Peale. *George Washington*. c. 1779–1781. Oil on canvas, 96 × 60" (241 × 156 cm).

Gilbert Stuart. *George Washington*. Begun 1795. Oil on canvas, 30¼ × 25¼" (76.8 × 64.1 cm).

John Singleton Copley. *Daniel Crommelin Verplanck*. 1771. Oil on canvas, 49½ × 40" (125.7 × 101.6 cm).

Ralph Earl. *Elijah Boardman*. 1789. Oil on canvas, 84 × 51" (210 × 129 cm).

James Peale. *Still Life: Balsam Apple and Vegetables*. c. 1820s. Oil on canvas, 20¼ × 26½" (51.4 × 67.3 cm).

Edward Hicks. *The Falls of Niagara.* c. 1825. Oil on canvas, 31½ × 38" (80 × 96.5 cm).

Thomas Cole. *View from Mount Holyoke, Northampton, Massachusetts, after a Thunderstorm–The Oxbow.* 1836. Oil on canvas, 50 × 74" (130.8 × 193 cm).

Frederic Edwin Church. *Heart of the Andes.* 1859. Oil on canvas, 5'6" × 10' (168 × 302 cm).

Albert Bierstadt. *The Rocky Mountains, Lander's Peak.* 1863. Oil on canvas, 72 × 102" (182 × 259 cm).

Lecture Nineteen

Eastman Johnson. *The Hatch Family.* 1870–1871. Oil on canvas, 48 × 74" (121.9 × 186.4 cm).

Alexander Roux. Cabinet. c. 1866. Rosewood, tulipwood, cherry, poplar, pine, 53 × 72 × 18" (135.6 × 186.4 × 46.7 cm).

Herter Brothers. Library Table. 1882. Rosewood, brass, mother-of-pearl, 31¼ × 60 × 35¾" (79.4 × 152.4 × 90.8 cm).

Augustus Saint-Gaudens. Vanderbilt Mantelpiece. c. 1881–1883. Marble, mosaic, oak, and cast iron, 15'4" × 13' × 3'1" (468 × 393 × 94 cm).

Louis Comfort Tiffany. Loggia from Laurelton Hall, Oyster Bay, New York. c. 1905. Limestone, ceramic, glass, 21 × 23' (640 × 701 cm).

Augustus Saint-Gaudens. *Hiawatha.* Modeled 1871–1872, carved 1874. Marble, 93 × 33 × 37" (236 × 87 × 94 cm).

———. *Diana.* 1893–1894, this cast 1894 or after. Bronze, 28¼ × 16¼ × 14" (71.8 × 41.3 × 35.6 cm).

Daniel Chester French. *The Angel of Death and the Sculptor* from the *Milmore Memorial.* 1889–1893, this version 1926. Marble, 93 × 100 × 32" (237 × 255 × 82 cm).

Thomas Eakins. *The Champion Single Sculls (Max Schmitt in a Single Scull).* 1871. Oil on canvas, 32¼ × 46¼" (81.9 × 117.5 cm).

Mary Cassatt. *The Cup of Tea.* c. 1880–1881. Oil on canvas, 36½ × 25¾" (92.4 × 65.4 cm).

John Singer Sargent. *Madame X (Madame Pierre Gautreau).* 1883–1884. Oil on canvas, 81 × 43" (208 x 109 cm).

James Abbott McNeill Whistler. *Arrangement in Flesh Colour and Black: Portrait of Théodore Duret.* 1883. Oil on canvas, 76 × 36" (193.4 × 90.8 cm).

John Henry Twachtman. *Arques-la-Bataille.* 1885. Oil on canvas, 60 × 78" (152 × 200 cm).

Childe Hassam. *Celia Thaxter's Garden, Isles of Shoals, Maine.* 1890. Oil on canvas, 17¾ × 21½" (45.1 × 54.6 cm).

William Merritt Chase. *At the Seaside.* c. 1892. Oil on canvas, 20 × 34" (50.8 × 86.4 cm).

Winslow Homer. *The Gulf Steam.* 1899. Oil on canvas, 28 × 49" (71.4 × 124.8 cm).

Lecture Twenty

Pablo Picasso. *Harlequin.* 1901. Oil on canvas, 32¾ × 24" (82.9 × 61.3 cm). Gift of Mr. and Mrs. John L. Loeb, 1960.

————. *Gertrude Stein.* 1906. Oil on canvas, 39½ × 32" (100 × 81.3 cm).

Jean-Auguste-Dominique Ingres. *Louis François Bertin.* 1832. Oil on canvas, 45¾ × 37½" (116 × 95 cm). Musée du Louvre, Paris.

Pablo Picasso. *Girl Reading at a Table.* 1934. Oil and enamel on canvas, 63 × 50" (162.2 × 130.5 cm).

Henri Matisse. *Nasturtiums with the Painting "Dance."* 1912. Oil on canvas, 74 × 44" (191.8 × 115.3 cm).

————. *Dance (I).* Early 1909. Oil on canvas, 8'6½" × 12'9½" (259 × 390 cm). Museum of Modern Art, New York.

Salvador Dalí. *The Accommodations of Desire.* 1929. Oil and cut-and-pasted printed paper on cardboard, 8¾ × 13¾" (22.2 × 34.9 cm).

Umberto Boccioni. *Antigraceful.* 1913, cast 1950–1951. Bronze, 23 × 20½ × 20" (58.4 × 52.1 × 50.8 cm).

Constantin Brancusi. *Bird in Space.* 1923. Marble, H (with base) 56¾" (144.1 cm), Diameter 6½" (16.5 cm).

Bastis Master (Attributed). Marble female figure. Early Cycladic II, late Spedos type. c. 2600–2400 B.C. Marble, H 24¾" (62.79 cm).

Gaston Lachaise. *Standing Woman (Elevation).* 1927. Bronze, 72 × 31 × 17" (185.1 × 81.3 × 45.1 cm).

Charles Demuth. *The Figure 5 in Gold.* 1928. Oil on cardboard, 35½ × 30" (90.2 × 76.2 cm).

Grant Wood. *The Midnight Ride of Paul Revere.* 1931. Oil on masonite, 30 × 40" (76.2 × 101.6 cm).

Georgia O'Keeffe. *Cow's Skull: Red, White, and Blue.* 1931. Oil on canvas, 40 × 36" (101.3 × 91.1 cm).

Balthus. *The Mountain.* 1936. Oil on canvas, 8' × 12' (248 × 365 cm).

Charles Rennie Mackintosh. Washstand. 1904. Oak, ceramic tile, colored and mirror glass, lead, 62 × 50 × 20" (160.7 × 130.2 × 51.8 cm).

Josef Hoffmann (designer). *Tea Service.* c. 1910. Silver, amethyst, carnelian, ebony. Various dimensions.

Ludwig Mies van der Rohe. "MR" Armchair. 1927. Tubular steel, painted caning, 31½ × 22 × 37" (80 × 55.9 × 94 cm).

Frank Lloyd Wright. Living room from the Little House, Wayzata, Minnesota. 1912–1914. 13'8" × 46' × 28' (4.17 × 14 × 8.53 m).

Lecture Twenty-One

Alberto Giacometti. *Three Men Walking (II).* 1949. Bronze, 30 × 13 × 12¾" (76.5 × 33 × 32.4 cm).

Max Beckmann. *Beginning.* 1949. Oil on canvas, 5'9" × 10'5" (175 × 318 cm).

Clyfford Still. *1947-8-W-No. 1(PH-114).* 1947–1948. Oil on canvas, 92 × 71" (233 × 179.7 cm).

Willem de Kooning. *Attic.* 1949. Oil, enamel, and newspaper transfer on canvas, 61 × 81" (157 × 205 cm).

Battle between Romans and Barbarians. The Portonaccio Sarcophagus. c. 180–190. Museo Nazionale Romano, Rome.

Jackson Pollock. *Autumn Rhythm (Number 30).* 1950. Enamel on canvas, 8'9" × 17'3" (266 × 525 cm).

Mark Rothko. *No. 13 (White, Red on Yellow).* 1958. Oil and acrylic with powdered pigments on canvas, 96 × 80" (242 × 206 cm).

Ellsworth Kelly. *Blue Green Red.* 1962–1963. Oil on canvas, 90 × 81" (231 × 208 cm).

Roy Lichtenstein. *Stepping Out.* 1978. Oil and magna on canvas, 84 × 69" (218 × 177 cm).

Fernand Léger. *The Three Musicians.* 1944 (after a drawing of 1924–1925; dated on painting 1924–1944). Oil on canvas, 68 × 56" (173.9 × 145 cm). The Museum of Modern Art, New York.

Andy Warhol. *Self-Portrait.* 1986. Acrylic and silkscreen on canvas, 79 × 79" (203 × 203 cm).

James Rosenquist. *House of Fire.* 1981. Oil on canvas, 6'6" × 16'6" (198 × 502 cm).

Romare Bearden. *The Block.* 1971. Cut and pasted printed, colored, and metallic papers, photostats, pencil, ink marker, gouache, watercolor, and pen and ink on masonite, overall 4' × 18' (121 × 548 cm), each of six panels 48 × 36" (121.9 × 91.4 cm).

Red Grooms. *Chance Encounter at 3 A.M.* 1984. Oil on canvas, 8'3" × 13' (254 × 393 cm).

Lecture Twenty-Two

Bernardo Daddi and The Assistant of Daddi. *The Assumption of the Virgin*, fragment of an altarpiece. c. 1340. Tempera on panel, gold ground, 42½ × 54" (108 × 136.8 cm).

Osservanza Master. *Saint Anthony the Abbot in the Wilderness.* c. 1435. Tempera and gold on panel, overall 18¾ × 13¾" (47.6 × 34.6 cm), painted surface 18½ × 13¼" (47 × 33.7 cm).

Sano di Pietro. *Saint Anthony Abbot Tormented by Demons.* c. 1435. Tempera and gold on panel, 18¾ × 13½" (47.5 × 34.3 cm). Yale University Art Gallery, New Haven, Connecticut.

Giovanni di Paolo. *The Creation of the World and the Expulsion from Paradise.* 1445. Tempera and gold on panel, 18¼ × 20½" (46.4 × 52.1 cm).

————. *Paradise.* Tempera and gold on canvas, transferred from wood, overall 18½ × 16" (47 × 40.6 cm), painted surface 17½ × 15" (44.5 × 38.4 cm).

Sandro Botticelli. *The Annunciation.* c. 1485. Tempera and gold on panel, 7½ × 12½" (19.1 × 31.4 cm).

Neroccio de' Landi. *Annunciation.* c. 1475–1480. Tempera on panel, 19½ × 50½" (49 × 128.5 cm). Yale University Art Gallery, New Haven, Connecticut.

Leonardo da Vinci. *Annunciation.* c. 1473–1475. Oil on panel, 39 × 84" (98 × 217 cm). Galleria degli Uffizi, Florence.

Hans Memling. *The Annunciation.* 1480–1489. Oil on panel, transferred to canvas, 30 × 21½" (76.5 × 54.6 cm).

Petrus Christus. *A Goldsmith in His Shop, Possibly Saint Eligius.* 1449. Oil on oak panel, overall 39½ × 33¾" (100.1 × 85.8 cm), painted surface 38¾ × 33½" (98 × 85.2 cm).

Quentin Metsys. *The Moneylender and His Wife.* 1514. Oil on board, 28 × 26¾" (71 × 68 cm). Musée du Louvre, Paris.

El Greco. *Saint Jerome as Cardinal.* c. 1610–1614. Oil on canvas, 42½ × 34¼" (108 × 87 cm).

Rembrandt van Rijn. *Portrait of Gérard de Lairesse.* 1665. Oil on canvas, 44½ × 34½" (112.7 × 87.6 cm).

———. *Self-portrait.* 1660. Oil on canvas, 31¾ × 26½" (80.3 × 67.3 cm).

Gerard de Lairesse. *Apollo and Aurora.* 1671. Oil on canvas, 80 × 76" (204 × 193 cm).

Francisco de Goya y Lucientes. *Condesa de Altamira and Her Daughter, María Augustina.* 1787–1788. Oil on canvas, 77 × 45" (195 × 115 cm).

Albrecht Dürer. *Self-portrait, Study of a Hand and a Pillow* (recto). 1493. Pen and brown ink, 11 × 8" (28 × 20 cm).

———. *Self-Portrait with Sea-Holly.* 1493. Oil on parchment on canvas, 22 × 17" (56.5 × 44.5) cm. Musée du Louvre, Paris.

———. *Six Pillows* (verso of *Self-portrait, Study of a Hand and a Pillow*). 1493. Pen and brown ink, 11 × 8" (28 × 20 cm).

Rogier van der Weyden. *The Annunciation.* c. 1435. Oil on panel, 34 × 36¾" (86 × 93 cm). Musée du Louvre, Paris.

Rembrandt van Rijn. Sketch after Leonardo da Vinci's fresco *The Last Supper.* c. 1635. Red chalk on buff prepared paper, 5 × 8" (12.4 × 20.9 cm).

Leonardo da Vinci. *The Last Supper.* 1498. Tempera on plaster, 15 × 29" (38.1 × 73.6 cm). S. Maria delle Grazie, Milan.

Canaletto. *Warwick Castle: The East Front.* 1752. Pen and brown ink, gray wash, 12½ × 22" (31.6 × 56.2 cm).

———. *Warwick Castle, East Front from the Courtyard.* 1752. 29½ × 48" (75 × 122 cm). Birmingham Museums & Art Gallery, Birmingham, Great Britain.

Domenico Tiepolo. *The Burial of Punchinello.* c. 1800. Pen and brown ink, brown and yellow wash, over black chalk, 14 × 18¾" (35.3 × 47.3 cm).

Bernaert van Orley (designer), Pieter de Pannemaker (probable weaver). *The Last Supper.* c. 1520–1530. Wool, silk, silver-gilt thread, 52' × 54'3" (1,584 × 1,653 cm).

Albrecht Dürer. *The Last Supper.* 1510. Woodcut, 15¾ × 11" (40 × 28 cm).

Lecture Twenty-Three

Jean-Auguste-Dominique Ingres. *Princesse de Broglie.* 1851–1853. Oil on canvas, 47¾ × 35¾" (121.3 × 90.8 cm).

Jean-Baptiste Camille Corot. *Diana and Actaeon.* 1836. Oil on canvas, 61½" × 44½" (156.2 × 113 cm).

Claude Monet. *Landscape at Zaandam.* 1871–1872. Oil on canvas, 18 × 26½" (45.7 × 67 cm).

Pierre-Auguste Renoir. *Two Young Girls at the Piano.* 1892. Oil on canvas, 44 × 34" (111.8 × 86.4 cm).

Henri Matisse. *Olive Trees at Collioure.* 1906. Oil on canvas, 17½ × 21¾" (44.5 × 55.2 cm).

André Derain. *Houses of Parliament at Night.* 1905–1906. Oil on canvas, 31 × 39" (78.7 × 99.1 cm), framed 40½ × 47½ × 3" (102.5 × 121 × 7.6 cm).

Claude Monet. *The Houses of Parliament (Effect of Fog).* 1903–1904. Oil on canvas, 32 × 36½" (81.3 × 92.4 cm).

Pierre Bonnard. *Before Dinner.* 1924. Oil on canvas, 35½ × 42" (90.2 × 106.7 cm).

Balthus. *Nude Before a Mirror.* 1955. Oil on canvas 75 × 64½" (899 × 772 cm).

Statue of an Offering Bearer. c. 1985 B.C. Dynasty 12, Middle Kingdom, Egyptian, Western Thebes. Gessoed and painted wood, H 44" (112.1 cm).

Jean-Auguste-Dominique Ingres. *Study of a Female Figure (Study for "Raphael and the Fornarina" [?]).* c. 1814. Pencil on white woven paper, 10 × 7¾" (25.4 × 19.7 cm).

————. *Raphael and the Fornarina.* 1814. Oil on canvas, 25½ × 21" (64.77 × 53.34). Fogg Art Museum, Cambridge, Massachusetts.

Raphael. *Madonna della Seggiola ("Madonna of the Chair").* c. 1516. Oil on panel, Diameter 28" (71 cm). Galleria Palatina, Palazzo Pitti, Florence.

Jean-François Millet. *Women Carrying Fagots.* c. 1858. Charcoal heightened with white gouache, charcoal border, on heavy gray-blue laid paper, 13½ × 10¾" (34.3 × 27.6 cm).

Edgar Degas. *Study of a Ballet Dancer* (recto) c. 1873. Oil paint heightened with body color on prepared pink paper, 17½ × 12½" (44.5 × 31.4 cm).

————. *A Woman Ironing.* 1873. Oil on canvas, 21½ ×x 15½" (54.3 × 39.1 cm).

————. *Two Dancers*. 1873. Dark brown wash and white gouache on bright pink commercially coated wove paper, now faded to pale pink, 24 × 15½" (61.3 × 39.4 cm).

Adolph von Menzel. *Studies of a Young Woman*. 1870 or 1879. Graphite on paper, 6¼ × 9½" (15.9 × 24.1 cm).

Pierre-Auguste Renoir. *Young Girl in a Blue Dress*. c. 1890. Watercolor with gouache highlights on thick cream wove paper, 8¼ × 6½" (20.8 × 16 cm).

Georges Seurat. *Study for "Les Poseuses."* 1886. Conté crayon on laid paper, 11¾ × 9" (29.7 × 22.5 cm).

Odilon Redon. *Pegasus and Bellerophon*. c. 1888. Charcoal, charcoal with water wash, white chalk, erasure highlighting on buff papier bueté, darkened, 21 × 14" (53.7 × 36.1 cm).

Felix Vallotton. *Street Scene in Paris*. 1895. Gouache and oil mounted on cardboard, 14 × 12" (36 × 30 cm).

Lecture Twenty-Four

Whose Sleeves? (Tagasode). Late 16th century. Ink, color, and gold on gilded paper, 22'5" × 53'8" (365 × 1,635 cm).

Rembrandt van Rijn. *Portrait of a Woman*. 1632. Oil on canvas, 44 × 35" (111.8 × 88.9 cm).

Paul Cézanne. *Mont Sainte-Victoire and the Viaduct of the Arc River Valley*. 1882–1885. Oil on canvas, 25¾ × 32" (65.4 × 81.6 cm).

Edgar Degas. *The Dancing Class*. Probably 1871. Oil on panel, 7¾ × 10¾" (19.7 × 27 cm).

Timeline

July 4, 1866	Paris meeting of Americans at the Bois de Boulogne in Paris, where they decide to create a "national institution and gallery of art" in America.
c. 1865	The Union League Club of New York, under the leadership of John Jay, works with political leaders, philanthropists, and art collectors to create the museum.
April 13, 1870	New York City leaders founded The Metropolitan Museum of Art; the museum's first accession, the Roman sarcophagus from Tarsus, donated.
1872	The museum opens to the public for the first time in the Dodworth Building at 681 Fifth Street.
1872	Artist John Kensett dies, leaving 38 paintings to the museum's collection.
1873	Museum moves to the Douglas Mansion at 128 West 14th Street; the museum purchases the Cesnola Collection from excavations in Cyprus.
1880	The museum moves to Central Park at 82nd Street and Fifth Avenue; Vanderbilt donates 670 Old Master drawings.
1886	The Department of Paintings established.
1889	Lucy W. Drexel and Mrs. John Crosby Brown make a large donation of musical instruments; the museum acquires two paintings by Édouard Manet.

1901 .... $7 million gift by Jacob S. Rogers creates a fund for the purchase of art.

1902 .... The Central Wing is finished and opens to the public.

1906 .... Museum starts undertaking archaeological expeditions to Egypt, financed by J. P. Morgan; the Department of Egyptian Art established; the George A. Hearn Fund created to purchase art from living artists.

1907 .... The museum acquires its first Renoir painting; the Department of European Sculpture and Decorative Arts established.

1909 .... The Department of Greek and Roman Art established.

1910 .... The museum becomes the first to include Matisse in its collection.

1911 .... The North Wing, designed by McKim, Mead and White, is completed.

1912 .... The Department of Arms and Armor established.

1913 .... The South Wing, designed by McKim, Mead and White, is completed; Benjamin Altman donates his collection of European paintings.

1915 .... The Department of Far Eastern Art is established.

1916 .... The Department of Prints created, with William M. Ivins, Jr. as its first curator.

1917 .... J. P. Morgan donates a large gift instrumental in developing the museum's medieval collection; a gift by

Isaac Fletcher creates the Fletcher Fund for acquisitions.

1925 .... John D. Rockefeller purchases sculpture from The Cloisters in order to donate it to the museum.

1926 .... The Beaux Art style facade and additions by Robert Morris Hunt are completed and open to the public.

1929 .... The H. O. Havemeyer bequest of Old Master and Impressionist paintings.

1931 .... The Michael Friedsam bequest.

1933 .... The Department of Medieval Art and The Cloisters established.

1934 .... The American Decorative Arts Department established.

1938 .... The Cloisters opens in Fort Tryon Park.

1946 .... The Stieglitz collection of photographs donated; the Museum of Costume Art merges with The Metropolitan Museum of Art.

1948 .... The Department of American Paintings and Sculpture established; the Department of Musical Instruments created.

1949 .... The Jules Bache collection of European painting is donated to the museum.

1956 .... The Department of Ancient Near East Art established.

1963 .... The Department of Islamic Art created.

1967 .... The Department of Contemporary Art established.

1969 .... Robert Lehman dies and leaves his art collection to the museum.

1970	Department of Contemporary Art incorporated into the new Department of 20th Century Art [Dept. of Modern Art].
1971	Approval of the museum's comprehensive architectural plan by architectural firm Kevin Roche, John Dinkeloo and Associates.
1975	The Lehman Wing housing the Lehman Collection opens to the public.
1978	The Sackler Wing is completed and the Temple of Dendur is installed; the Treasures of Tutankhamun temporary exhibition.
1980	The completion of the American Wing with 24 period rooms.
1981	The Astor Court and the Douglas Dillon Galleries of Chinese paintings open to the public; the Mr. and Mrs. Charles Wrightsman bequest.
1982	The Rockefeller Wing opens; the Department of the Arts of Africa, Oceania, and the Americas established.
1987	The Lila Acheson Wallace and Henry R. Kravis wings created; the Ford Motor Company and John C. Waddell donate their large photograph collection.
1991	The completion of the museum's comprehensive architectural plan.
1992	The Department of Photographs established.
1993	The Department of Drawings and Prints established; the Blanche and A. L. Levine Court opens.

1994 .... The Florence and Herbert Irving Galleries open.

1996 .... The Robert and Renée Belfer Court opens.

1997 .... The Gilman Gallery opens, dedicated to displaying photographs.

1998 .... The Arts of Korea gallery installed.

1999 .... The renovated galleries of the Department of Near Eastern Art reopen.

2000 .... The Cypriot Galleries open.

2007 .... The reinstalled Greco-Roman galleries reopen.

Glossary

altarpiece: A piece of art—in most cases a series of paintings or sculpture on panel—to be positioned behind or above an altar.

Annunciation: The biblical narrative in which the angel Gabriel announces the miraculous incarnation to the Virgin Mary.

avant-garde: French for "fore guard" (referring to soldiers who advanced at the front of an army unit). A term used to describe art or artists that are at the front of a movement or that are experimental and innovative.

calligraphy: Specialized decorative hand lettering using a brush or pen.

composition: A principle of design referring to the arrangement or placement of elements in a work of art.

cuneiform: Pictographic writing elements inscribed in clay tablets; typically created in ancient Mesopotamia.

diptych: A two-paneled piece of art often joined together by hinges and used as an altarpiece.

donor: An individual or single business entity that financially supports or donates to an institution such as a church or a museum.

engraving: A printing method in which an incising tool or graver is used to cut an image into the surface of a metal plate. Ink is applied to the incised surface and wiped off, leaving ink in the wells of the incisions; a print is then created using this inked plate.

etching: A type of print where an image is drawn with an etching needle onto a chemically treated metal plate, which is then put into a chemical acid bath that etches or bites into the lines of the drawn image. Ink is then placed into these etched depressions, and the plate is used to create a printed impression.

genre: The term used to describe the depiction of ordinary, common life and activities.

icon: Considered sacred in and of itself, an icon is a pictorial representation of a sacred figure or event painted on a wooden panel or surface.

iconography: The study of the pictorial representation of the collected images or representations of a particular subject or subject matter.

illumination: Images or decorations, typically with brilliant colors and metals, used to enrich the text and letters of manuscripts or writings.

kouros: Greek for "young man," this term refers to the idealized youth depicted in classical sculpture.

krater: A large bowl from ancient Greece or Rome with a wide mouth and two vertical handles, normally used for mixing wine and water.

manuscript: A handwritten document or book typically created before the invention of printing.

mihrab: A niche in the wall of an Islamic mosque that indicates the direction of Mecca.

oil painting: The art or technique of painting with oil colors, which are pigments suspended in a drying medium (such as linseed oil).

parable: An allegorical story or statement meant to teach a moral lesson or religious principle.

Passion: The theological term referring to the narrative of Christ's sufferings from the Last Supper through the Crucifixion.

pietà: The visual representation of the Virgin Mary holding and mourning over the dead body of Christ.

plein air: The type of painting executed outdoors and directly responding to what is in front of the artist.

polychrome: An object such as a statue, vase, or mural in which a variety of colors has been used.

reliquary: A receptacle or repository for sacred relics.

sarcophagus: A stone coffin, typically having inscriptions or decorative sculpture.

stele: An upright slab or stone bearing inscriptions upon its surface, used as a monument or a commemoration.

still life: The visual representation of an inanimate object or series of inanimate objects.

tempera: A type of water-based paint in which ground pigment is suspended in egg yolk.

terracotta: Latin for "earth cooked," this term refers to a hard, semi-fired, waterproof, brownish-orange clay used in pottery.

triptych: Greek for "threefold," this term refers to a series of three panels of paintings usually hinged together.

woodcut: A type of print where an image is cut in relief onto the "plank" part of a piece of wood; ink is applied to create an image from this matrix.

Biographical Notes

Altman, Benjamin (1840–1913): An early donor to the museum who bequeathed important paintings by artists like Boticelli and Rembrandt.

Annenberg, Walter and Leonore (1908–2002; b. 1918): Long supporters of the museum, their gifts include the Annenberg Collection of Impressionist and Postimpressionist Paintings and a $20 million grant to purchase art works.

Bache, Jules (1861–1944): Donated important works of art in 1949, including works by Crivelli, van Dyck, and Goya.

Cesnola, Luigi Palma di (1832–1904): The museum's first director.

Clark, Stephen (1882–1960): Former trustee and donor who gave works including Seurat's *Circus Sideshow* and Degas's *The Singer in Green* (c. 1884).

de Montebello, Philippe (b. 1936): The museum's current director. He has improved the quality of both the museum and its galleries and has made a series of extraordinary acquisitions.

Havemeyer, H. O. and Louisine (1847–1907; 1885–1929): Generous donors to who gave paintings such as El Greco's *View of Toledo* and a very large and important collection of Impressionist paintings in 1929.

Hoving, Thomas (b. 1931): The museum's director from 1966 until 1977.

Hunt, Richard Morris (1828–1895): Architect of the museum's 1926 Beaux Art façade and additions.

Jay, John (1817–1894): Proposed that a "national institution and gallery of art" be created. His later efforts brought together New York City leaders and art enthusiasts, eventually giving birth to the museum.

Johnston, John Taylor (1820–1893): Railroad tycoon and the museum's first president. His personal art collection was the core of the museum's collection.

Lehman, Robert (1891–1969): New York banker who donated about 3,000 works of art to the museum that are housed in the Lehman Wing.

Morgan, J. P. (1837–1913): Philanthropist and museum trustee from 1903 to 1913, he generously donated art work to the museum including period rooms and the Raphael's *Madonna and Child Enthroned with Saints*.

Mould, Jacob Wrey (1825–1886): The architect of the original red brick building along with Calvert Vaux, which housed the museum's collection along Fifth Avenue in Central Park.

Putnam, George Palmer (1814–1872): The New York publisher who became the museum's founding superintendent.

Rockefeller, John D. (1839–1937): Philanthropist and early supporter of the museum who acquired and donated many works of art, including The Cloisters.

Rockefeller, Michael C. (1938–1964): An anthropologist and the youngest son of Nelson A. Rockefeller, he was memorialized in the Michael C. Rockefeller Wing dedicated to the arts of Africa, Oceania, and the Americas.

Rockefeller, Nelson A. (1908–1979): Benefactor who donated over 3,000 pieces of art to the museum in memory of his son, Michael C. Rockefeller.

Rorimer, James J. (1905–1966): Director of the museum from 1955 to 1966.

Sage, Mrs. Russell (1828–1918): Collector of early American furniture and objects whose donation of almost 900 pieces established the core of the museum's Department of American Decorative Arts.

The Vanderbilts: Various members of the Vanderbilt family have contributed many works of art to the museum, including Cornelius Vanderbilt (1794–1877), who donated 670 old master drawings, and William K. Vanderbilt (1878–1944), who donated Rembrandt's 1632 painting, *Man in Oriental Costume ("The Noble Slav")*.

Vaux, Calvert (1824–1895): The museum's architect who designed the red brick Central Park building along with Jacob Wrey Mould.

Wrightsman, Charles and Jayne: Recent museum donors who gave paintings by artists such as Vermeer and Rubens in honor of the museum's curators.

Bibliography

Aldred, Cyril. *Temple of Dendur*. New York: Metropolitan Museum of Art, 1978.

Allen, James P. *The Heqanakht Papyri: Publications of the Metropolitan Museum of Art Egyptian Expedition, 27*. New York: Metropolitan Museum of Art, 2004.

Auchincloss, Louis. *J. P. Morgan: The Financier as Collector*. New York: Abrams, 1990.

Avery, Kevin J., and Peter L. Fodera. *John Vanderlyn's Panoramic View of the Palace and Gardens of Versailles.* New York: Metropolitan Museum of Art, 1988.

Baetjer, Katharine. *European Paintings in the Metropolitan Museum of Art by Artists Born Before 1865: A Summary Catalogue.* New York: Metropolitan Museum of Art, 1980.

Barnhart, Richard. *Asia (The Metropolitan Museum of Art Series).* New York: Metropolitan Museum of Art, 1987.

Bean, Jacob. *100 Drawings in the Metropolitan Museum of Art.* New York: Metropolitan Museum of Art, 1964.

Behrendt Kurt A. *The Art of Gandhara in The Metropolitan Museum of Art.* New Haven: Yale University Press, 2006.

Bolger, Doreen. *American Pastels in the Metropolitan Museum of Art.* New York: Abrams, 1989.

Brettell, Richard, Francoise Forster-Hahn, Duncan Robinson, and Janis Tomlinson. *The Robert Lehman Collection at the Metropolitan Museum of Art, Volume IX: Nineteenth- and Twentieth-Century European Drawings.* New York: Metropolitan Museum of Art, 2002.

Brooks, Sarah T. *Byzantium: Faith and Power (1261–1557): Perspectives on Late Byzantine Art and Culture: The Metropolitan Museum of Art Symposia.* New York: Metropolitan Museum of Art, 2007.

Caldwell, John, Oswaldo Rodriguez Roque, Dale T. Johnson, and Kathleen Luhrs. *American Paintings in The Metropolitan Museum of Art, Vol. 1.* New York: Metropolitan Museum of Art, 1994.

Capistrano-Baker, Florina H. *Art of Island Southeast Asia: The Fred and Rita Richman Collection in the Metropolitan Museum of Art.* New York: Metropolitan Museum of Art, 1994.

Clark, Kenneth. *Masterpieces of Fifty Centuries: Metropolitan Museum of Art.* New York: E. P. Dutton, 1970.

Collins, Lisa Gail, and Lisa Mintz Messinger. *African-American Artists, 1929–1945: Prints, Drawings, and Paintings in The Metropolitan Museum of Art.* New York: Metropolitan Museum of Art, 2003.

Cone, Polly. *The Jack and Belle Linsky Collection in The Metropolitan Museum of Art.* New York: Metropolitan Museum of Art, 1984.

D'Alton, Martina. "The New York Obelisk, or How Cleopatra's Needle Came to New York and What Happened When It Got Here" *The Metropolitan Museum of Art Bulletin*, 4.72 (Spring 1993).

Danziger, Danny. *Museum: Behind the Scenes at the Metropolitan Museum of Art.* New York: Viking, 2007.

Dean, Bashford. *Helmets And Body Armor In Modern Warfare: The Metropolitan Museum Of Art.* New York: Metropolitan Museum of Art, 2007.

de Montebello, Philippe. *Met and the New Millennium: Chronicle of the Past and a Blueprint for the Future.* New York: Metropolitan Museum of Art, 1994.

———. *The Metropolitan Museum of Art Guide Revised Edition.* New York: Metropolitan Museum of Art, 2007.

———, and Barbara Burn. *Masterpieces of the Metropolitan Museum of Art.* New York: Metropolitan Museum of Art, 1993.

Dorman, Peter F. *The Metropolitan Museum of Art: Egypt and the Ancient Near East.* New York: Metropolitan Museum of Art, 1987.

Douglas, Newton. *Art of Africa, the Pacific Islands, and the Americas.* New York: Metropolitan Museum of Art, 1980.

Druesedow, Jean L. "Celebrating Fifty Years of the Costume Institute." *The Metropolitan Museum of Art Bulletin*, 4.64 (Fall 1987).

Frelinghuysen, Alice Cooney. *Splendid Legacy: The Havemeyer Collection.* New York: Metropolitan Museum of Art, 1993.

Galitzn, Kathryn Calley, and Gary Tinterow. *Masterpieces of European Painting in the Metropolitan Museum of Art, 1800–1920.* New York: Metropolitan Museum of Art, 2007.

Gardner, Albert Ten Eyck, and Stuart P. Feld. *American Paintings: Catalogue of the Collection of the Metropolitan Museum of Art I: Painters Born by 1815.* New York: Metropolitan Museum of Art, 1965.

Grancsay, Stephen V. *Loan Exhibition of Mediaeval and Renaissance Arms and Armor from the Metropolitan Museum of Art.* Los Angeles: Los Angeles County Museum, 1953.

Grinnell, Isabel Hoopes. *Greek Temples.* New York: Metropolitan Museum of Art, 1943.

Hambourg, Maria Morris. "Photography between Wars: Selections from the Ford Motor Company Collection." *The Metropolitan Museum of Art Bulletin*, 4.56 (Spring 1988).

Hartt, Frederick. *The Metropolitan Museum of Art: Renaissance in Italy and Spain.* New York: Metropolitan Museum of Art, 1987.

Heckscher, Morrison H. *American Furniture in the Metropolitan Museum of Art: Late Colonial Period: The Queen Anne and Chippendale Styles.* New York: Metropolitan Museum of Art, 1986.

———. *The Metropolitan Museum of Art: An Architectural History.* New York: Metropolitan Museum of Art, 1995.

Hibbard, Howard. *Metropolitan Museum of Art.* New York: Metropolitan Museum of Art, 1980.

Hindman, Sandra, Mirella Levi D'Ancona, Pia Palladino, and Maria Francesca Saffiotti. *The Robert Lehman Collection at the Metropolitan Museum of Art.* Princeton: Princeton University Press, 1998.

Hoving, Thomas. *The Chase and Capture: Collecting at the Metropolitan.* New York: Metropolitan Museum of Art, 1975.

———. *Making the Mummies Dance: Inside the Metropolitan Museum of Art.* New York: Simon and Schuster, 1993.

Howard, Kathleen, ed. *Metropolitan Museum of Art.* New York: Metropolitan Museum of Art, 1983.

Ivins, William Mills. *Prints and Books: Informal Papers.* New York: Metropolitan Museum of Art, 1926.

Kisluk-Grosheide, Danielle, Wolfram Koeppe, and William Rieder. *Highlights of the European Furniture Collection.* New Haven: Yale University Press, 2006.

Kjellgren, Eric. *Oceania: Art of the Pacific Islands in The Metropolitan Museum of Art.* New York: Metropolitan Museum of Art, 2007.

Koda, Harold, Andrew Bolton, and Mimi Hellman. *Dangerous Liaisons: Fashion and Furniture in the Eighteenth Century.* New York: Metropolitan Museum of Art, 2006.

LaGamma, Alisa. *Art and Oracle: African Art and Rituals of Divination*. New York: Metropolitan Museum of Art, 2000.

————. *Echoing Images: Couples in African Sculpture*. New York: Metropolitan Museum of Art, 2004.

————. *Eternal Ancestors: The Art of the Central African Reliquary*. New York: Metropolitan Museum of Art, 2007.

Lerman, Leo. *Museum: One Hundred Years and the Metropolitan Museum of Art*. New York: Viking Press, 1969.

Libin, Laurence. *Our Tuneful Heritage: American Musical Instruments from The Metropolitan Museum of Art*. New York: Metropolitan Museum of Art, 1998.

Lieberman, William S. *Painters in Paris: 1895–1950*. New York: Metropolitan Museum of Art, 2000.

————, Lisa Mintz Messinger, Sabine Rewald, and Lowery S. Sims. *20th Century Art Painting 1945–85: Selections from the Collection of the Metropolitan Museum of Art*. New York: Metropolitan Museum of Art, 1987.

Liebling, Roslyn, Christine Lilyquist, Thomas J. Logan, and Karen Briggs. *Time Line of Culture in the Nile Valley and Its Relationship to Other World Cultures*. New York: Metropolitan Museum of Art, 1978.

Liedtke, Walter. *Dutch Paintings in The Metropolitan Museum of Art*. New York: Metropolitan Museum of Art, 2007.

————. *Flemish Paintings in the Metropolitan Museum of Art Two Volumes*. New York: Metropolitan Museum of Art, 1984.

Little, Charles T. *Set in Stone: The Face in Medieval Sculpture*. New Haven: Yale University Press, 2006.

Luhrs, Kathleen, ed. *American Paintings in the Metropolitan Museum of Art*. New York: Metropolitan Museum of Art, 1980.

Marandel, J. Patrice. *Europe in the Age of Enlightenment and Revolution (The Metropolitan Museum of Art Series)*. New York: Metropolitan Museum of Art, 1987.

Martin, Richard. *Our New Clothes: Acquisitions of the 1990s*. New York: Metropolitan Museum of Art, 1999.

McCann, Anna Marguerite. *Roman Sarcophagi in the Metropolitan Museum of Art*. New York: Metropolitan Museum of Art, 1978.

Mertens, Joan. *Greece and Rome*. New York: Metropolitan Museum of Art, 1987.

Milleker, Elizabeth J., and Joseph Coscia. *Light on Stone: Greek and Roman Sculpture in The Metropolitan Museum of Art: A Photographic Essay*. New York: Metropolitan Museum of Art, 2004.

Miller, R. Craig. *Modern Design in the Metropolitan Museum of Art, 1890–1990*. New York: Metropolitan Museum of Art, 1990.

Moffett, Charles S. *Impressionist and Post-Impressionist Paintings in the Metropolitan Museum of Art*. New York: Metropolitan Museum of Art, 1998.

Muscarella, Oscar White. *Bronze and Iron: Ancient Near Eastern Artifacts in the Metropolitan Museum of Art*. New York: Metropolitan Museum of Art, 1988.

Naef, Weston J. *The Collection of Alfred Stieglitz: Fifty Pioneers of Modern Photography*. New York: Metropolitan Museum of Art, 1978.

Nickel, Helmut, Stuart W. Pyhrr, and Leonid Tarassuk. *Art of Chivalry: European Arms and Armor from the Metropolitan Museum of Art: An Exhibition*. New York: Metropolitan Museum of Art, 1982.

Norris, Michael, Carlos A. Picon, Joan R. Mertens, and Elizabeth J. Milleker. *Greek Art from Prehistoric to Classical: A Resource for Educators*. New York: Metropolitan Museum of Art, 2001.

O'Neill, John P., ed. *20th Century Art: Selections from the Collection of the Metropolitan Museum of Art*. New York: Metropolitan Museum of Art, 1986.

———. *Mexico: Splendors of Thirty Centuries*. New York: Metropolitan Museum of Art, 1990.

Peck, Amelia. *Period Rooms in the Metropolitan Museum of Art*. New York: Metropolitan Museum of Art, 1996.

Phipps, Richard, and Richard Wink. *Invitation to the Gallery: An Introduction to Art*. New York: Metropolitan Museum of Art, 1987.

Picón, Carlos, and Richard De Puma. *Art of the Classical World in the Metropolitan Museum of Art: Greece, Cyprus, Etruria, and Rome*. New York: Metropolitan Museum of Art, 2007.

Pittman, Holly. *Art of the Bronze Age: Southeastern Iran, Western Central Asia, and the Indus Valley*. New York: Metropolitan Museum of Art, 1984.

———. *Egypt and the Ancient Near East*. New York: Metropolitan Museum of Art, 1987.

Pope-Hennesy, John. *The Study and Criticism of Italian Sculpture.* New York: Metropolitan Museum of Art, 1980.

Pyhrr, Stuart W., Donald J. LaRocca, and Morihiro Ogawa. *Arms and Armor: Notable Acquisitions 1991–2002.* New York: Metropolitan Museum of Art, 2003.

Quodbach, Esmee. *The Age of Rembrandt: Dutch Paintings in The Metropolitan Museum of Art.* New York: Metropolitan Museum of Art, 2007.

Richardson, Joy. *Inside the Museum: A Children's Guide to the Metropolitan Museum of Art.* New York: Harry N. Abrams, 1993.

Roque, Oswaldo R. *The United States of America (The Metropolitan Museum of Art Series).* New York: Metropolitan Museum of Art, 1987.

Rousseau, Theodore. *Guide to the Picture Galleries.* New York: Metropolitan Museum of Art, 1954.

Russell, John Malcolm. *From Nineveh to New York: The Strange Story of the Assyrian Reliefs in the Metropolitan Museum and the Hidden Masterpiece at Canford.* New York: Metropolitan Museum of Art, 1997.

Salinger, Margaretta. *Masterpieces of American Painting in the Metropolitan Museum of Art.* New York: Metropolitan Museum of Art, 1986.

Scully, Vincent Joseph. *New World Visions of Household Gods & Sacred Places: American Art and the Metropolitan Museum of Art, 1650–1914.* New York: Metropolitan Museum of Art, 1988.

Sims, Lowery Stokes, Sabine Rewald, and William S. Lieberman. *Still Life: The Object in American Art, 1915–1995: Selections from the Metropolitan Museum of Art.* New York: Metropolitan Museum of Art, 1996.

Snyder, James. *The Renaissance in the North.* New York: Metropolitan Museum of Art, 1987.

Stauffer, Annemarie, Marsha Hill, Helen C. Evans, and Daniel Walker. *Textiles of Late Antiquity.* New York: Metropolitan Museum of Art, 1995.

Szabó, George. *Masterpieces of Italian Drawing in the Robert Lehman Collection, the Metropolitan Museum of Art.* New York: Metropolitan Museum of Art, 1983.

———. *The Robert Lehman Collection: A Guide.* New York: Metropolitan Museum of Art, 1975.

Thompson, Nancy. *Roman Art: A Resource for Educators.* New York: Metropolitan Museum of Art, 2007.

Tinterow, Gary. *Modern Europe.* New York: Metropolitan Museum of Art, 1980.

———. *The New Nineteenth-Century European Paintings and Sculpture Galleries.* New York: Metropolitan Museum of Art, 1993.

Tomkins, Calvin. *Merchants and Masterpieces: The Story of the Metropolitan Museum of Art.* New York: Dutton, 1970.

Valenstein, Suzanne G. *Handbook of Chinese Ceramics.* New York: Metropolitan Museum of Art, 1975.

Von Bothmer, Dietrich. *The Metropolitan Museum of Art Guide to the Collections: Greek and Roman Art.* New York: Metropolitan Museum of Art, 1964.

Von Sonnenburg, Hubert. *Rembrandt/Not Rembrandt: In The Metropolitan Museum of Art—Aspects of Connoisseurship.* New York: Metropolitan Museum of Art, 1995.

Watt, James C. Y., An Jiayao, Angela Falco Howard, and Boris I. Marshak. *China: Dawn of a Golden Age, 200–750 AD.* New York: Metropolitan Museum of Art, 2004.

Weitzenhoffer, Frances. *Havemeyers: Impressionism Comes to America.* New York: Metropolitan Museum of Art, 1986.

Welch, Stuart. *The Islamic World.* New York: Metropolitan Museum of Art, 1987.

Winlock, Herbert Eustis, and Harry Burton. *The Tomb of Queen Meryet-Amun at Thebes: The Metropolitan Museum Of Art Egyptian Expedition.* New York: Metropolitan Museum of Art, 1972.

Zeri, Federico, and Elizabeth E. Gardner. *Italian Paintings: A Catalogue of the Collection of the Metropolitan Museum of Art, North Italian School.* New York: Metropolitan Museum of Art, 1986.

———. *Italian Paintings: A Catalogue of the Collection of the Metropolitan Museum of Art, Sienese and Central Italian Schools.* New York: Metropolitan Museum of Art, 1980.

Recommended Web Sites:

The general information website for The Metropolitan Museum of Art is www.metmuseum.org. It contains a variety of information including free downloadable podcasts of select objects in the museum's collection, a visitor site with all the useful information for planning a visit, and a link to sign up for a membership to receive regular mailings and special member benefits.